FROM 60 YARDS IN

1817

HARPER & ROW, PUBLISHERS, New York
Grand Rapids, Philadelphia, St. Louis, San Francisco
London, Singapore, Sydney, Tokyo

FROM 60 · YARDS IN ·

*How to Master Golf's
Short Game*

RAY FLOYD

with Larry Dennis

FIRST EDITION

Designed by Nina D'Amario
Illustrations by Ken Lewis
Photographs © 1989 by Tony Roberts

Library of Congress Cataloging-in-Publication Data

Floyd, Ray.
   From 60 yards in: how to master golf's short game/by Ray Floyd with Larry Dennis.—1st ed.
      p. cm.
   ISBN 0-06-016075-6
   1. Short game (Golf) I. Dennis, Larry, 1933– . II. Title.
III. Title: From sixty yards in.
GV979.S54F56   1989   796.352′3—dc19   88-45510

89 90 91 92 93 CC/RRD 10 9 8 7 6 5 4 3 2 1

CONTENTS

INTRODUCTION

A Look at Ray Floyd

A remarkable fellow, Raymond Floyd.

I sat with him in the cramped locker room at Shinnecock Hills, the lovely lady of Long Island and the only U.S. Open course Floyd has ever liked. He was pulling on his shoes for the final round. We talked idly, about magazines and baseball—which he will talk about only if you let him—and other trivia. It was June 15, 1986. Floyd, after an opening 75, had quietly sneaked up the leaderboard and was three strokes behind. But nobody was paying attention.

Floyd had won only one tournament in three and a half seasons. He wasn't exactly on his last legs. He had been the number-five money-winner in 1985. But he had blown the Westchester Classic the week before in totally un-Floydlike fashion, and some heads were shaking. He was 43 years, 9 months, 11 days old. Nobody that old had ever won a United States Open.

Then he went out and won the Open. He shot 66 to beat the most tightly bunched final-round field in Open history on one of its finest courses. Then he cried.

Ray Floyd the golfer is far from unknown. Ray Floyd the person is ... well, *undetected* might be a good way to put it. That's mainly because he prefers it that way.

In 25 years on the PGA Tour he has won 21 or 22 tournaments, depending on whether you believe the Tour's count or his. Four of those have been major championships, two PGAs and a Masters to go along with the Open. In 1983 he won the Vardon Trophy, awarded to the player with the lowest scoring average on Tour. He was nominated for the World Golf Hall of Fame in 1988. He didn't make it on the first ballot, but he'll get there soon.

He also has won more than $3 million in official money and a whole lot more unofficially, which is important only if you're trying to make a living.

His peers see him as a money player, the supreme compliment from that fraternity, and as a leader. Floyd has played on six United States Ryder Cup teams. The Professional Golfers Association has named him captain of the 1989 team, an appointment not lightly given or lightly accepted. Raymond considers it perhaps his greatest honor. It is a signal indication of the man's stature in the golf world . . . and of how far he has come.

Floyd's early career is well chronicled—maybe too well. He was taught by his father, L. B. Floyd, a career soldier and a golf professional who ran a driving range near Fort Bragg, North Carolina, and later owned his own course. Raymond Floyd won the International Jaycee Junior Championship in 1960 at the age of 17. He accepted the first golf scholarship ever awarded by the University of North Carolina, then dropped out of school after three months. After an 18-month stretch in the army, Floyd joined the PGA Tour in 1963 and, in his eleventh professional start, won the St. Petersburg Open. At the age of 20½, he was the youngest man to win a professional event since the 1920s and the fourth youngest ever to win one.

Floyd was named *Golf Digest*'s Rookie of the Year, and stardom was imminent. At which time he promptly became the playboy of, if not the western world, at least the PGA Tour. He enjoyed a pretty girl or two, a drink or three, and baseball more than golf, it seemed. He did not win again until the 1965 St. Paul Open, then not again for three years after that. His life-style was blamed, but Floyd insists that "I was fortunate to win as soon as I did. There weren't nearly as many good players then. It wasn't until three years later that I felt I could compete against anybody."

Whatever. In the fall of 1968, he had a talk with Mark McCormack of International Management Group, Floyd's new agent.

"Mark pointed out that if I continued to go the way I had been, I would have a mediocre career," Floyd says. "He told me I should set some goals, so I sat back and did just that."

The goals he set were a Ryder Cup berth, a major championship, and $100,000 in winnings, a steep mountain in those days. So in 1969 he won three tournaments, including the PGA Championship, and $109,957.

When Raymond Floyd sets goals, he takes them seriously.

The trouble was, he didn't set any more for a while. "I lost my desire to play golf," he says. "Goals didn't seem important." And he didn't win again for six years.

Goals are important to Maria Fraietta, a successful businesswoman who owns fashion and design schools. She is a striking beauty with brains and a will that could stare down Attila the Hun. Floyd met and married her in 1973, and she turned his life around. Since then she has given birth to three children and Raymond Floyd's new career.

Early on, Maria looked her husband in the eye and said, "If you don't want to play golf, get into something else that would interest you. But don't waste your life."

"That shook me up," says Floyd.

Must have. He has gone from there to the threshold of the Hall of Fame.

Credit Maria, but don't forget Ray Floyd. She provided the spark. He fanned the flame of a fire that was always there, smoldering.

"I decided to see how good I could be," he says.

We know how good he has been on the golf course. What most of the world doesn't know is how good he has been outside the ropes.

Floyd is a Tour loyalist. He served on the Tournament Policy Board for two years and did, by consensus of his peers, a hell of a job. He plays regularly in lesser tournaments never graced by other superstars.

"I know when tournaments are hurting for a field," he says. "So instead of taking a week off, I go and play."

He is good with fans, especially the young ones. He signs autographs where and when others don't. He does charity appearances. He does good deeds that few hear about. I won't detail them here, because he doesn't care if they are recognized. He derives his own satisfaction. He is remembering what got him where he is, and he is paying back.

"I used to be a taker," he says. "Now I like to think I'm a giver."

That usually presents a dilemma, a conflict between the two things he loves most in life, his family and golf.

"I am basically a very selfish person," Floyd says. "My family is first and foremost. Golf is second. But things keep coming up that you know you should do, because they are charitable, or because they go along with being the U.S. Open champion, or because they are part of putting something back into the game you love. When I do these things, it takes time from my family."

It's the price of superstardom, of course, but Floyd does not complain. And he knows how to handle it. Whether it is Maria, maturity, or mental toughness—and it probably is a combination of all these—he has his life sorted out.

Careful attention to your preputt routine pays off on the green.

Much has been written and said about the Ray Floyd "look"—the bulging eyes and the glaze that comes over them when he is on the trail of a victory. Maria said that when she saw that look on the tenth hole at Shinnecock, when Floyd was still two strokes behind, she knew the Open was history.

Floyd brings the same intensity to anything he does, including this book. I did not spend as much time with him as I have with others on books of this nature, but I didn't have to. Raymond uses every hour efficiently, and he gets that same look in his eyes.

"The mind is a limitless commodity," he says. "With practice in using it correctly, you can do anything you want."

The gospel according to Floyd takes that far beyond writing books.

"If you set a goal and if you have a burning desire to accomplish that goal," he says, "if you program yourself and visualize yourself getting there and if you are strongly committed, you will make it. There may be detours. Life has a way of testing you, of finding out if you really want it. If you do, you get around the obstacle and go ahead. You have to put in a lot of effort.

"Nothing I have ever accomplished has been easy for me. I always have had to work hard. I don't have a classic golf swing. I have to practice. I really don't like to practice. But I like the results I get because I practice."

Remember that last line. Raymond will talk a lot about practice in the pages that follow.

He will talk about the subject he knows as well as any man in the world—how to get your ball up and down from any situation. Jim Murray, the syndicated columnist for the *Los Angeles Times* who does words better than most of us dream of, once put it best: "Floyd could one-putt a swamp and get the ball out of an ocean with backspin on it."

This book might not help you do that, but when you finish you will know everything about getting out of more conventional hazards.

One of the beauties of the book is that Floyd is not dogmatic about his instruction. He does not teach a method. He realizes what every good player and teacher has discovered, that golf is an individual game and that the successful swing, whether it is short or long, must be tailored to each person's physical characteristics and abilities. He is a stickler for fundamentals. He believes,

Ray Floyd holds
the 1986 U.S. Open
trophy.

rightly so, that without the proper foundation nobody can play the game consistently well. He will give you his fundamentals, his preferences, but he will tell you to experiment until you have arranged them to suit yourself.

Most exciting is that you will get into Raymond Floyd's mind, and he will get into yours. That alone is worth the price of the book. If he never described a shot, his observations on the mind and its applications would help you play better golf.

This is an honest book. It does not try to tell you that golf is an easy game. As Floyd himself says, "I had to play it a while before I found out how hard it is."

It is also an entertaining book, shot through with anecdotes from Floyd's career. If you don't care to heed his instructions, to pay whatever price is necessary for improvement, you still will have fun reading it.

But I think Floyd will convince you that the quickest and easiest way to lower your score is to heighten your emphasis on the short shots. My wife, Lynn, a 10-handicapper with a pretty good short game of her own, copyread the manuscript. When she finished, she immediately headed for the club to try out his ideas.

Raymond and I hope you will be equally inspired.

—Larry Dennis
Huntington, Connecticut
October 1988

1

GOLF AND THE MIND
An Overview

At its highest level, on the professional tours, golf is being played better today than ever before. There are many theories that account for this—the ball goes farther, the clubs are better, the players are stronger—all of which may have some validity. My own theory, and I can substantiate it pretty well, is that so many players are making so many low scores because they are superb around and on the greens.

I don't think players today are the shot makers, with the full swings, that we had when I started playing. Mostly they just beat it long and, hopefully, straight. But they are artists with the wedge, the chipping clubs, and the putter. Why? Because they have to be to survive.

Everybody today just goes for the flag. I think the all-exempt Tour has something to do with that attitude—players don't have to worry about making the cut and playing next week. But they also don't worry about missing the green. They are fearless, because there is no such thing as an impossible recovery shot as far as they are concerned.

It used to be that if you faced a difficult bunker shot, you more or less conceded bogey. Not anymore. Now you have to find a way to get the ball close or you lose a lot of ground to the field. So every player on Tour has improved his bunker play in the last several years, out of necessity. And it's the same with every other recovery shot.

Look at the PGA Tour statistics. The best player out here hits about 70 percent of the greens in regulation over the course of the season. When you get below the top 10, the numbers start sliding toward 60 percent pretty rapidly. That means most players are hitting between 10 and 13 greens a round. Yet everybody is shooting par or better—those who aren't don't stay around very long. Which means they are getting it up and down a lot of times every day.

For one thing, we're playing much tougher courses these days—longer, more heavily bunkered, more difficult in all respects around the greens. That means we don't hit as many greens, so there is more need to make great recoveries. And that's fine with me. I like the trouble shots, especially the short ones, the little finesse shots, the shots you have to create to get the ball close enough for a makable putt. That's the greatest pleasure in the game as far as I'm concerned.

I think I'm a good competitor. And while I guess my swing is not classic, I think I can hit all the shots with the best of them. But my career has been as good as it has because of my short game. I'm in my twenty-seventh year on Tour, and what has kept me so highly competitive all these years has been my proficiency from 60 yards in.

After I won the U.S. Open at Shinnecock Hills in 1986, I went into a bit of a slump. There were a lot of demands on my time, and I let them take precedence over my golf game. I didn't allow enough time for practice. I particularly neglected my short game. The rest of my game remained relatively okay. I was driving the ball and hitting the irons as I normally do. But the recovery shots were not getting as close and the putts were not going in as often, so my scores were going up and my income was going down. This is not an excuse; it's a statement of fact. I had fallen down in the most important area of the game.

That's the dumbest thing I could have done, and I know better. I won the Open with my short game, on one day, in fact. In the opening round on Thursday we played in what may have been the worst weather I've ever encountered—cold, rainy, and the wind howling on a course that had few trees for protection and is one of the world's most difficult. I had no feel whatsoever for the full shots and hit them terribly. I had a double-bogey and two unplayable lies during the round. I shot 75, and while that doesn't sound very good, that's the round that won the Championship for me. I finished only five shots behind the leader on a day when the average score was 78.1. And mine could have been 85. I took only 25 putts. My pitching, chipping, and putting saved me.

In the 1988 PGA Championship at Oak Tree in Edmond, Oklahoma, I holed three chip shots during the first round, then made a near-impossible chip shot from the rough on the thirteenth hole for a birdie in the second round. I also made a 172-yard hole-in-one during the third round, but I guess we can't count that as a chip-in.

A streak like that is unusual, of course, but the point is that it made up for a lot of errors. I didn't win the championship, but those four chip shots holed made the difference between finishing tied for ninth with five others and tying for thirty-first with seven others. It meant the difference between earning $21,500 and $4,842, which is a pretty big difference in anybody's paycheck. And it might have made an even bigger difference had I taken three shots to get down on any of them instead of being lucky enough to put them in the hole. And when I say lucky, I mean that there is of course a certain amount of luck in sinking a shot from off the green. But all were very good shots and would have finished around the hole in any event. I just gave them a chance to go in, and they did.

The week after the PGA, at The International in Colorado, I chipped in again. I guess that sort of thing goes in cycles, but I do chip in a lot. I'll average chipping in once a tournament, at least every four or five rounds. That may not sound like much, but go back over your last season and see how many times you did it. For me, and for any Tour player, the saving of one stroke a tournament can make a big difference in the money total at the end of the year. Occasionally it can mean the difference between winning a tournament and not winning.

If the short shots, then, are important to the professionals, they are doubly important to the amateurs. I don't have any statistics to back up this statement (I suspect nobody else does, either), but I'd bet that very few amateurs hit half the greens in regulation in

With proper technique, a short chip is just like a
medium-length putt and can be holed.

a given round. Even the good amateurs I see, the single-figure
handicappers and the guys who score in the 70s most of the time,
depend on their short games to score well. They miss a lot of
greens but they are good pitchers, chippers, and putters, and so
they don't make a lot of bogeys.

I don't think there is any specific way to play golf, so there is
no specific way to putt, chip, or pitch the ball. Golf, to me, basically is a game of feel, and the philosophies I express in this book

come from the feel that I've developed over the years. I will give you the fundamentals, as I see them, but I strongly urge you to take those fundamentals and build your own swing, your own short-game shots, your own putting stroke—something you can *feel* when you are on the golf course. If you know the feel that works and can recapture it when you're playing, you won't have to worry about the ABCs, the mechanics, every time you step up to the ball. And you will be a much better player for it.

I'm going to dwell on the mental aspects of this game. Once you have a swing or a stroke that works reasonably well, your mental and emotional approach becomes about 95 percent of the package that determines how well and how consistently you score. That's a well-known, often-published, often-discussed fact, but too many amateurs, as well as a few professionals, don't pay attention. At least they seem to forget it as soon as they hit the first tee. Then they resume worrying about their setups, their grips, their backswings, and all the other facets of the swing. Once they start that, they forget the reason they're out there, which is to advance the ball and get it into the hole in the fewest number of strokes. They are not *playing* golf.

Here's an example of playing golf that I'm sure you can relate to, because at some time or another it has happened to you, perhaps without your realizing it. Think back to a time when you were buried deep in the woods. There was only a narrow opening in front of you, you had to keep the ball low to avoid overhanging branches, and you had to hit it hard and hook it to get it into the fairway and let it roll onto the green. And you did it, probably without thinking about it. How did that happen? Reflect back on your mental processes at the moment. You probably were concerned with *what* you had to do with the shot, not *how* you were going to do it. You weren't worrying about your technique, about the swing you were going to make. You simply saw where you had to hit the ball and you hit it there. You were playing golf.

That leads to a phenomenon that I will bring up often in this book—*visualization.* It has been called "going to the movies," and it may be the most important part of your mental package. It is one of the most critical factors involved in playing golf well.

In 1981, I had a one-stroke lead over David Graham going to the seventy-second hole of the Doral-Eastern Open. There is not a harder driving hole on earth than the eighteenth on Doral's Blue

Course, a 437-yard par-4 with a lake running all the way down the left. The wind was from the left and against us, from the northeast, the most difficult wind you can face. It wasn't exactly a situation that engendered a lot of confidence.

I walked on the tee and suddenly I had the most comfortable sensation, the feeling that I was going to hit a perfect drive. I looked down the hole and I "saw" this beautiful drive going out there with a little draw just off the right corner of the lake. I swung the club and it was the most beautiful feeling I can remember. It was ecstasy, just like the easiest practice swing I had ever made. I looked up and the ball was going like a rifle shot down the

When in trouble, visualize the shot flying out rather than worrying about your swing.

middle of the fairway with a little draw, right around the corner of the lake. I drove it farther than was possible against that wind. Then I hit a 4-iron to the back of the green and walked off with the title.

That sort of thing had happened to me before and has happened since. The feeling is one of seeing everything happen before it happens, or as if it already has happened and you are just doing it again. It's as if you are playing from films. It most often happens in putting, but it can happen at any other time. Often it's on a particular shot. I have pulled off shots in near-impossible situations where I literally could see beforehand what was going to happen—I had to drive the shot into the ground, bounce it over a trap, and run it up a bank and down the green to the hole. And it happened.

Sometimes the feeling lasts for a round, sometimes for an entire tournament. In the 1976 Masters, in which I tied the tournament record of 271 and won easily, I played every shot in my mind from the first tee to the last putt on the seventy-second green. I had the feeling throughout the 1982 PGA Championship.

That's the fun part . . . I mean, the *really* fun part. I used to question it, wonder why it was happening. Then I learned not to question it, simply to accept that it was happening and enjoy it.

Why does that feeling come over me? Why did I know I was going to hit that perfect drive? Why did I know the recovery shot was going to come off, the putt was going to fall? I suspect it was a combination of my confidence in my ability and my concentration on what I had to do.

That confidence and that ability to concentrate on the shot come from practice and experience. I'm playing back the thousands of putts, chips, pitches, and all the other shots I've hit over the years. They're a reflection of the positive experiences I've had.

I think a player can induce a preview, a visualization, of a shot. The mind does control the body, and if you work hard at controlling your mind, using it in the right way, you can produce the proper response from your muscles. If you concentrate, you can see the putt rolling into the hole, see the pitch shot floating high over the bunker and settling close to the hole.

It happens in all sports. I used to watch Dwight Stones, an Olympic high-jump champion and former world record holder, as he prepared for a jump. He stood as if in a trance, but you could

see his head bobbing and his eyes moving down the line toward
the bar. He was tracing his steps in advance, visualizing every
move he would make during the jump.

But it is impossible to induce or visualize a shot that you cannot
perform, that you have not performed countless times in the past.
If you are a 100-shooter who has played for 2 years, or if you have
played for 20 years once a week or twice a month and have never
practiced, you have nothing in the bank to draw on. You have no
positive experiences to play back.

As you may have heard, I'm a great baseball fan, especially of
the Chicago Cubs. I'd love to be able to pitch for the Cubs in the
last game of the World Series and throw a knuckleball past Jose
Canseco for the final out to preserve the championship. The problem is, I don't even know how to grip a knuckleball. I can watch
Charlie Hough, a fine knuckleball pitcher for years, throw one,
but that doesn't help me. If Charlie were to show me how to grip
a knuckleball and I started throwing them every day, maybe in a
year or two I could throw a pretty good one. Then it would be up
to the Cubs to get into a World Series.

That's why I'm also going to emphasize practice (on the short
game, not the knuckleball) in this book. Practice lets you build
and refine your swing and gives you the experiences you can then
call on during a round of golf. A lot of golfers, who do other things
for a living, don't like to be told to practice. All they want to do is
go out and play and enjoy themselves, to have a relaxing walk in
the park and spend time with friends. And there is nothing wrong
with that. That's why golf is such a great game. You can approach
it any way you want and still enjoy it. But if you enjoy competition,
if you want to be as good as you can be, you're going to have to do
a certain amount of work on the range. Every good shot you hit
on the practice tee, every putt you hole on the practice green, goes
into your memory bank, your computer. Similarly, every time you
hole a putt on a course anywhere in the world, you have something more to refer to the next time you encounter that putt somewhere else—and you always will. You get better each time until
finally you say to yourself, subconsciously, "Hey, I've got confidence in this shot and I can make it."

I can't make you practice, nor do I want to. You have to make
yourself do it. Whether you realize it, you choose the level at
which you play. If you want to play better than you do now, get

to the practice tee or practice bunker or putting green. Preferably, take your professional along, because he or she can help you. But get there. It's the only way to develop the muscle memory in your swing or putting stroke so that you can repeat it most of the time on the course.

This physical competence, at whatever level you can achieve

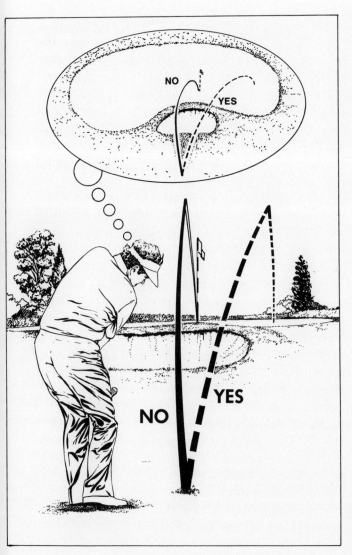

The safe,
high-percentage shot
often is away from the
flagstick.

through the combination of practice and your inherent talent, frees you to do what you must to make the best number, to visualize the shot or the putt, to play the game better and make it more fun at the same time.

It produces the positive attitude I will stress in the following chapters. I don't know of a successful player who doesn't approach each shot with the idea in his mind that he can make the shot, with confidence and trust in his game. That holds true at any level. I have a good friend at Indian Creek, my home club in Miami. He's an amateur and a very good putter. He rarely, if ever, practices, other than to hit a few putts before he tees off. But his confidence is so good, he has been a good putter for such a long time, that he never thinks about it. I suspect that at one point in his life he worked on his putting a lot, but now it's second nature to him and he continues to be a good putter without practice. That's because he believes in himself. He says, "I'm a good putter," so he is.

With confidence comes mental toughness that helps you handle pressure situations. And we all have those, whether it's the U.S. Open Championship or a $2 Nassau on the line. If you believe in yourself, in your ability, you can cope and succeed.

Late in 1986, after I had won the U.S. Open, I came to the seventy-second hole of the Walt Disney/Oldsmobile Classic needing a birdie to tie Lon Hinkle and Mike Sullivan, who had already finished. Standing in the fairway I told my caddie, "Just get me on the green and I can make it." I hit the shot 18 feet from the hole. Now, most people think the hardest putt to make is the one to win, but it's really the putt you have to tie. If you miss, you lose. I said to myself, "I'm a professional, and here's a chance to tie." And I got the job done. I hit the putt right in the middle of the hole. Then I came out of a bunker and made a 7-footer to win the tournament on the first playoff hole.

You are what you think you are, in golf and in life. You can be whatever you want to be. And you can beat whoever you want to beat, if you work at it and put your mind in the proper frame. I've never wanted to go against anybody I didn't think I could beat. The feeling in the pit of your stomach just isn't going to allow you to play well.

I've gone into competition feeling like I wasn't going to win.

And I didn't. I've gone into competition knowing I couldn't be beaten, and I've won. I've also gone into competition with that same feeling and have lost. But I've never been beaten badly in that state of mind, and I've never beaten myself. I've always been competitive under those circumstances.

I think the best example of the psychological impact of confidence on a golfer is the Senior Tour. Look at the dozens of players who go out there after mediocre careers on the regular Tour and suddenly blossom into stars. Sure, the competition is not as deep and the courses are set up a little shorter and easier. But they start *playing* better, probably better than they ever have in their lives.

Chi Chi Rodriguez was one of the worst putters I've ever seen, and he admits it. Then he goes onto the Senior Tour and holes everything. Orville Moody, who may have been *the* worst putter I've known at our level of competition, suddenly starts making putts and a ton of money.

Sure, Chi Chi got a widely publicized lesson from Bob Toski and Orville went to the new long putter and a different method. But the real difference is that they and the others who have played well got a new attitude. All of a sudden they are not playing against Curtis Strange and Greg Norman and Joey Sindelar and Paul Azinger and Mark Calcavecchia and the other young stars. Now they are again playing against guys whom they used to beat or were competitive with. And there aren't as many of them. On the regular Tour, when you miss a putt or shoot a mediocre score, 30 guys go past you. On the Senior Tour, you might drop a place in the standings, so each putt becomes relatively not as important. Also, there is no 36-hole cut, which takes a lot of pressure off during the first two rounds. And the players on the Senior Tour enjoy more camaraderie, approaching the game and the competition on a more relaxed basis. This is a second chance, a Mulligan they didn't expect, and they are enjoying it. So suddenly the yips are gone, the tension is out of the swing, and the birdies come again.

That is by no means a put-down of the Senior Tour. I think it's the greatest thing in the world for those guys. I'll probably be out there myself when the time comes. It's just a matter of once again finding their competitive level and regaining their confidence, their trust in themselves.

A good analogy can be seen in race horses. Let's say you claim a horse for $12,000 and drop him back into an $8,000 claiming race. He'll win easily and set a six-furlong track record, say 1:09. Then put him in a race with $20,000 horses. The race might be won in 1:10 and your horse won't finish. He has to be pulled up early. Why? The horse knows where he belongs. Psychologically he knows he can't run with those horses because they are better than he is, so he ties up. And don't shake your head. I've seen it happen too many times to doubt it.

This is not to say you can't *raise* your competitive level. I'm assuming you are not one of the 200 or 300 best players in the world, or you would be on Tour and not reading this book. At your level, whether it be club, local, state, or national competition, it is always possible to improve. The purpose of this book is to help you do just that. And believe me, improving your short game is the quickest way to cut strokes off your score and raise your competitive ability to that new level.

What I am saying is that you must be comfortable with your ability at whatever level you are playing. You must trust it, be positive about it, and not doubt yourself. This trust lets you play in a relaxed manner, free of tension. Relaxation, that light, supple feeling in your muscles, is the key to good ball striking and shot making. It is important on the full shots and even more so on the delicate chips and pitches and the critical putts. Once doubt creeps in, your muscles tighten, your mind goes awry, and you will never play to your potential, whatever that is at the moment.

You eliminate doubt by practice, by honing your physical skills to the point that you know they will work on the course. So practice and the mental aspect are forever entwined. I won't let you forget it throughout the rest of this book.

Please don't confuse doubt with nervousness. I don't know of any good player, from Jack Nicklaus on down, who isn't nervous when he goes out to play a competitive round of golf, whether it's in the second round of the Pensacola Open or the final round of the U.S. Open. In fact, I think I'd be worried if I didn't have a case of nerves before I played. It would mean I didn't care, that I wasn't pumped up enough to be competitive. At that point, I'm sure I wouldn't play very well.

I'll never forget my first Masters in 1965. Of course, growing up in the southeast as I did, the Masters was *the* tournament for me. When I walked onto the first tee in the first round and bent down to put the tee in the ground, my hand was shaking so badly I just knew I couldn't balance that ball on the tee. I'm sure it wasn't as noticeable to everyone else as I thought, but it was a dreadful experience for me. When I finally got the ball sitting on the tee, I was so thankful I didn't care where the drive went. Maybe that's why it went straight.

Years later, when I was a savvy veteran and was in contention for the title at Augusta, I tried to beat the traffic and arrived early for the final round, all suave and collected. I talked with reporters, got my balls for the round from my locker, broke out a new glove, and finally walked out to get my caddie. We went to the practice tee, where I unzipped my bag to put away my watch and the balls and prepared to hit my warm-up shots. It was only then that I realized I was still in my street shoes. The wily old fox, like everyone else, had a case of tournament nerves.

The secret is that you don't succumb to the nervousness. Everybody feels pressure, on the first tee and on the eighteenth green, especially if he's in contention. It's when you let the pressure affect your play that you have choked.

I go right back to the positive attitude, to the trust in my ability, as the way to prevent the nerves from taking over. The butterflies may flutter around a lot during a round, but they will only bother you if you let them, if you begin to doubt yourself. Just remember that no matter how critical the situation, you have hit this shot or made this putt before and you can do it this time.

When you get into a pressure situation, it is almost always because you are playing well. If you weren't, you would be so far behind in the tournament or so far behind in the bets that the next shot wouldn't matter anyway. So if your ability that day has gotten you this far, trust it to carry you farther. Concentrate not on what the shot means but on what you have to do to pull it off. Let the consequences take care of themselves.

There is a further antidote to nerves, which is to realize that no golf shot is a matter of life or death. At the amateur level, it isn't even a matter of income, unless you're betting more money than you can afford to lose. Cary Middlecoff, who is in the Hall of Fame, once said he relieved pressure on an important shot by telling himself, "If I miss the shot, my wife will still love me and I'll still have steak for dinner tonight."

I couldn't agree more. Golf is, after all, just a game, even if you make your living at it.

It becomes a matter of perspective. In the mid-1960s, I played the Caribbean Tour for a while. All the invited American players would travel together, and one day we were taking off from Bogotá, Colombia. The airport sat in sort of a bowl ringed by mountains, and we were packed into an old Constellation aircraft that was a little suspect. There wasn't enough room in the baggage compartment for all the gear, so we had golf bags stuffed in the aisle. We were definitely overloaded, but we all assumed that the pilot knew what he was doing and wouldn't try to take off if the plane wasn't safe.

As soon as we got settled on board, I started playing gin rummy with Al Besselink, a flamboyant guy who was seldom bothered by anything. The pilot taxied the plane to the end of the runway, made a U-turn, and revved the engines so hard I thought all the rivets were going to pop out. Then he cut the brakes loose and we started lumbering down the runway. It wasn't long before everybody on the plane got dead quiet, and Bessie turned dead white. We all realized we had been on the ground a long time. The plane was not going up.

Then there was a little give as the wheels left the ground— certainly it was far from the surge you normally feel when a plane takes off. I looked out the window and saw a herd of cattle in a pasture at the end of the runway. This was their permanent home and they were used to airplanes, but now they were stampeding. The plane had missed them by inches, and at the moment we were heading right into a mountain.

The pilot did get the plane turned at the last possible instant. Then he had to circle inside the bowl three times before he could get enough altitude to fly over the mountains.

At that point, a drive over water or a 5-foot putt, no matter how much money was involved, became a lot easier.

You also will reduce strokes if you play intelligently as well as confidently. Be aware of your limitations and don't try to exceed them. Play aggressively if you know the shot is in your arsenal, but if you can't feather a high, soft lob over a bunker to a close-cut pin, if you haven't practiced that shot enough to be sure of pulling it off the great majority of the time, then forget it and pitch to the center of the green. Give yourself some leeway. That's not playing defensively. That's playing wisely.

Which brings us to gambling—when should you and when should you not. I'm not talking about betting. I'm talking about trying dangerous shots to make a better score . . . and risk making a much worse one.

There is more opportunity, and more reason, to gamble in match play, which is what most amateurs play, than in stroke play, which is basically our game on Tour. For example, if your opponent is on the green in two and you are sure he is going to make par and you have a very difficult third shot over a bunker, then you must try to feather a high, soft shot onto the green and get it close. Never mind that it might not be your best shot, or even a shot that you have pulled off very often. You have no choice, and if you miss, all you've done is lost the hole.

But, if you are in a stroke-play tournament, you should simply try to get the ball on the green and accept the fact that you're going to have to make a 25-footer for a par. At least you can two-putt for a sure bogey.

Personally, I think that if you would play golf for score, considering everything stroke play instead of match play, you would have a lower handicap. And you would be a better player, because your mind would have to work a little better.

How many times have you accepted the fact that you had to chip out of the woods and take an extra stroke, then knocked it on the green and made a putt for par? On the other hand, how many times have you tried to play an impossible shot through the trees and wound up putting the ball in your pocket when you could have made no worse than bogey on the hole?

A 20-foot putt is certainly not impossible to make, but too many amateurs—and some professionals—think that if they don't gamble and knock the ball close they don't have a chance to make par. So they walk away with double-bogey or worse.

Gambling at the Tour level is different than at the club level. If I risk a high lob over a bunker and fall short, the recovery shot from sand probably won't be difficult for me, whereas it will be for most amateur players. So it is not as great a gamble for me.

But no matter how good a shotmaker you might be, there is a time to gamble and a time not to in stroke play. For example, let's say I'm playing the tenth hole of the final round of a tournament and I'm tied for the lead. The pin is on a platform at the rear of the green and I have just hit a beautiful second shot that has just trickled over the green and down a steep bank that has very little grass on it. Now, I can't possibly get a pitch shot close to the hole. The only way I can get my ball close is to putt it up the bank or bang a low shot into it and hope it bounces up. But if I don't hit it hard enough, the ball will roll right back down and I'll be looking at the same shot again.

At this point, I'm going to pitch the ball, even though I know I can't get it closer than 30 feet, and accept my bogey. I'm not about to make a double- or triple-bogey that would put me out of contention. I have time to make up one stroke, but not two or three.

If this same situation were to occur on the eighteenth hole and I needed par to tie, then I would gamble, of course. I wouldn't gamble, however, if I needed par to win. Then I'd pitch the ball and try to make the long putt for a par, but I'd make sure I at least got my bogey and made it into the playoff, where I still had a chance to win.

That's the stroke-play mentality, but let's apply it to match play. Think back to the times you've been playing in your club or city tournament and had a gamble backfire. Your opponent is on the green and needs a two-putt for par and you have to make that risky shot over the bunker and you fail. Then he three-putts and doesn't make par. Or your opponent drives the ball 240 yards down the middle and you hit it into the woods. He has an 8-iron left to the green and you can either chip out or try to hit your ball through a little opening in the trees. You gamble and fail. Your ball goes deeper into the woods and now you're dead. Now he hits his second shot in the creek and makes double-bogey. If you had played it safe, you would have won the hole. Has that ever happened to you? I'll bet it has.

I call it the Golfing Gods. Your opponent knocked it in the creek just to show you what a fool you were. Well, maybe not, but it seems that way often.

So think stroke play, not match. You'll be a better player and you will also win more matches.

The intelligent approach to golf includes planning your round. If it's important enough to you, spend time visualizing how you are going to play each hole. Sam Snead once told about how he used to imagine playing Augusta National the night before a round at the Masters. He would always break 60 in his mind. "I sure as hell wasn't going to practice shooting 80," he said with a smile. Well, he never broke 60, but he won three Masters titles, so I guess his method worked for him. It doesn't work that well for me. If I mentally practice hitting a perfect drive and then hit a bad one, my system gets scrambled. But it's something with which you might want to experiment.

I do planning of a different kind. When I'm at a tournament, I stay in my hotel room after dinner. I call home to talk to my wife and kids; then I think about how I'm going to play the next round. I go over it hole by hole, like a pitcher going over the hitters he will face in the next game. I keep a notebook in which I analyze shots I hit in earlier rounds or previous tournaments, and I study it.

For example, the eighteenth hole at LaCosta, site of the Tournament of Champions, had given me fits for years. It's a long par-4 that usually plays into the wind. The shape of the hole calls for teeing the ball on the left side, but I would invariably block my drive to the right and end up in trouble. One night I wondered what would happen if I teed up on the right side instead. I had to convince myself to do this, and I must have hit 50 drives from the right side in my hotel room that evening. When I came to the hole the next day, I was ready. It worked, and I haven't had any trouble with it since.

I suspect you might not keep notes of your previous rounds, nor do you probably lie awake nights imagining how you are going to play your next round. But I'll assure you that the more time you spend planning and visualizing, the better you will play.

If nothing else, by knowing and planning what you *can* do and avoiding the foolish mistake of trying to do what you *cannot,* you will save a lot of strokes in the long run. A lot of good rounds are ruined by players trying to exceed their capabilities.

I know that all too well. I've lost at least four major championships over the years by making mental mistakes in the final round. I would press, trying to exceed my limitations, and make a bogey. I was trying to make up ground instead of playing it one shot at a time, as I usually try to do.

Each time, I would realize afterward that if I had just been patient I probably would have won, because the players in front of me were making mistakes and backing up too. But I guess it takes a long time to learn.

As a matter of fact, it does take a long time. Most of us start this game at a 10 level physically but about a 1 level mentally. Our physical level drops as the years go on, but our mental ability increases so that, somewhere along the line, the two meet. Jack Nicklaus is the only man I know who started his career as a 10 both physically and mentally. The rest of us have to get smarter as we get older.

And we can, fortunately. So can you, and if you do, you will play better golf even as the bones start to creak a little and the tee shots get shorter and shorter. When you begin to realize that you can't knock down trees or hit balls 300 yards over the corner of a dogleg, you have matured as a player. You know your game and your capabilities. As long as your mind and your short game get sharper and sharper, your scores will get lower.

However, no matter how good you get or think you are, never expect perfection. Nobody has ever achieved it, especially in golf. If you stub a chip shot or miss a putt you think you should have made, shake it off and go on to the next hole. If you make a mental error, and you will, accept it and tuck it away in your mind, programming yourself to help prevent it from happening again.

Believe me, it happens to all of us, both the physical and mental mistakes. In the final round of the 1982 PGA Championship at Southern Hills in Tulsa I came to the eighteenth hole, a long and difficult par-4, with the title well in hand. I needed a par to break the tournament record, a bogey to tie it. I hit a perfect drive. Then I started rehearsing my acceptance speech. I hit my second shot into the rough short and right of the green, dumped my third into a bunker, came out and two-putted for a double-bogey six.

I still won easily, and maybe the record wasn't that important, but I was still kicking myself for not paying attention.

But that's going to happen, if only because we're all human. When it does, keep your mind and your approach to the game on an even keel. Stay positive. The next shot will be better.

Finally, I'm going to give you some advice that will help your golf game and your life, and it's really counsel that I shouldn't have to give.

Get your body in shape.

I neglected mine during the early part of my career, and it hurt me, especially since I'm a big man who can get overweight pretty easily. But in the last several years I've worked at physical conditioning, and it has paid big dividends. My eating and sleeping habits are better. I used to enjoy quite a bit of the grape. Now I don't drink at all when I'm playing. At home, I'll just have a little wine.

I was one of the first Tour professionals to use the Diversified Products fitness trailer when it began to appear at all the tournaments in 1985. Some of the guys laughed at me, especially some older, established players who wouldn't think of trying something like that. Let them laugh. I laugh at the pay window.

I wish we hadn't been in the Stone Ages as far as exercise is concerned when I started playing 30 years ago. When I was a youngster, weight lifting and that sort of thing were taboo for a golfer. My dad wouldn't even let me swim. Coaches thought you couldn't play golf and baseball at the same time, although I did both.

Now we know that proper weight training, along with stretching exercise, improves your strength and increases your elasticity. It has only been in the last few years that we've become sophisticated on the subject.

I work out at home as well as on Tour. I do an hour a day on the treadmill, exercise bicycle, and rowing machine. I do rotator cuff exercises with light weights, exercises for the lower back, and stretching exercises. I'm going to expand my routine gradually, because I'm sold on the benefits.

You should be too. Maybe you can't work out for an hour or two each day, but you can take enough time to shed a few pounds and tone up the muscles. Being physically fit only makes you feel better, live your life better, live longer, and play golf better. Nothing important, right?

The increased flexibility you get from doing the right exercises—and you'll have to check with your doctor or a fitness expert to find what is best for you—is especially important in golf. You can hit the ball farther, and you get a fluidness in the muscles that also helps on the short shots.

Basically, it comes down to the old business of a sound mind in a sound body. If you are physically fit, your nerves are better. And, wow, are we all looking for better nerves!

That's because we are all trying to play golf better. I hope the approach to the game that I have given you in this chapter and the instruction that follows will help you do just that.

OVERVIEW IN BRIEF

- Improving your short game is the quickest way to reduce your score.
- Tailor the fundamentals to fit your preferences.
- The mind controls the body—visualize; be confident, positive, and relaxed; trust your ability.
- Practice—physical competence breeds the correct mental approach.
- Accept the fact that you will be nervous; control nervousness with positive thoughts.
- Play intelligently; plan and visualize your round beforehand.
- Adopt the stroke-play mentality; you will lower your handicap and even win more matches.
- Accept the bad shots and the mental errors and stay on an even keel.
- Exercise to improve your physical condition; it will improve your nerves and your game.

2

PUTTING BASICS
The Way to Lower Scores

Putting well is the key to scoring well, which is really what golf is all about. As I have pointed out, nobody is going to hit all the fairways and greens. And no matter how good you become at chipping, pitching, and sand play, you're never going to hit every shot to within a foot of the cup. The putt is always the final stroke on every hole; in essence, it becomes the most important stroke. If you do not putt well, it matters very little how well you do the rest of the game. You might be a decent player, but you will never become as good as you could be. Every player on Tour is a marvelous striker of the ball. The players winning the tournaments and the most money also are marvelous putters.

Conversely, good putting can make up for a lot of sins committed from tee to green. You can hack it all over the lot, within reason, but if you can make putts you will put good numbers on the scorecard and collect a lot of bets in the grill room.

The strange thing is that putting is often downplayed. We have players on Tour who come in and tell you how well they hit the ball but how badly they scored. I suppose that's the macho instinct. Each is saying, "I'm a great ball hitter but I just can't get it in the hole."

I don't agree with that approach, probably because I know how important putting is. If somebody were to ask me how I would like to be remembered as a golfer, I'd say I want to be known as the greatest putter who ever lived. I'm sure that will never be my epitaph, but I'd like to be in the top 10. Throughout my career, putting has been one of my strong points. I would not have lasted as long as I have without it.

Sometimes, when I'm putting badly, my wife, Maria, will ask what is wrong. I'll say, "It's just a bad streak. I'm a good putter. I'll get it back."

That's not boasting. I *am* a good putter. I know it and I believe it. If I didn't believe it, as I'll discuss further in this chapter, I wouldn't be a good putter. And I'd be doing something else for a living.

Because of the importance of good putting, and because the mental approach you use on the green should be used everywhere else on the course, we're going to spend a lot of time in this chapter on putting. The chapter is divided into two principal sections, the first dealing with how to get ready to putt, how to establish the fundamentals of grip, setup, and stroke, the second dealing with the elements that go into making putts consistently.

Please bear with me as you wade through the first part. Just as every tall building must have a strong foundation, every good putter must have a solid knowledge of the fundamentals so he can best apply them to his own game.

After that we'll get into the fun part.

HOW TO PREPARE

Putting has a personality all its own. It is the most individualistic part of the game. Every time you walk into a golf shop you see 50 different kinds of putters. When you walk onto the putting green, you see many different grips, many different stances. There is no set way. But there are a few basics that you should observe. Within that fundamental structure, your putting method can be as personal as you want it to be, as long as it works. It's up to you to establish a position at the ball, a position with the putter in your hands that feels comfortable, that builds confidence, sending a signal to your brain that says, "I'm going to be able to make a good stroke and a successful putt."

The Grip

There are several basic grips in golf—the Vardon or overlapping grip, the interlocking grip, and the 10-finger grip normally are used for shots other than putting; the reverse overlap grip, with several variations, is the grip most used for putting; the cross-handed putting grip has been adopted by many players in recent years.

Any of these grips can be, and sometimes are, used for putting. I don't really recommend any one of them. As I said earlier, golf is a game of feel, and that's especially true in putting. You might want to experiment, especially if your putting goes bad for a while. I've experimented all my life with all segments of my golf game. Your body changes. Your feel changes. From day to day, things don't stay the same.

Personal preferences also vary. Gary Player likes to have his hands as close together as possible on the putter handle. He is trying to make them work as one. Ed Fiori, on the other hand, spreads his hands over as much of the handle as possible without actually separating them. Again, figure out what feels best and works best for you.

I'll explain here how to form the grips most commonly used in putting. The others will be discussed in the chapter that deals with pitching. The instructions are for right-handed players. Left-handers should simply reverse the directions.

The Reverse Overlap   The reverse overlap is considered the

most fundamentally sound grip for putting, and it's the grip I use. To assume the grip, take the following steps:

● Place your left hand on the club, positioning the handle against the top of the heel pad. The handle should run diagonally from the heel pad to a point between the bottom and second joints of your middle finger. The last three fingers of the left hand now close around the handle, and the heel pad acts as a vise, holding the club securely. The hand should be placed so the V formed by the thumb and forefinger is pointing up your left arm, generally toward your left shoulder. This is a little more "open" or turned to the left than the normal Vardon grip used for other shots. The thumb runs pretty much straight down the top of the handle, perhaps angling slightly toward the left shoulder. The forefinger at this point is still off the club.

● Place all four fingers of the right hand on the handle, basically along the pad at the base of the fingers, with the forefinger crooked around the handle. The little finger of the right hand should be resting snugly against the middle finger of the left. The right-hand V formed by the thumb and forefinger should be running straight up the right arm, about to the right shoulder or even slightly outside it. The right thumb is on top of the club, angling toward the right shoulder or slightly outside it.

● There are three ways now to deal with the reverse overlap: take that left forefinger that is still floating free and crook it around the little finger of the right, or crook it around the ring finger of the right, thus overlapping the last two fingers, or run it straight down across all the fingers of the right.

The Grip for Chipping and Putting. The same grip is used for chipping and putting—the reverse overlap, in which the forefinger of the left hand is set over the fingers of the right, with the two hands positioned in opposition.

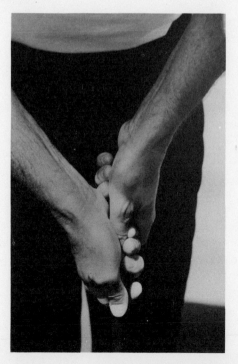

Any of these methods works. Experiment to find which feels comfortable for you . . . and which helps you get the ball in the hole most often.

A variation of this grip is the double reverse overlap, in which the ring finger of the right hand is snuggled up against the middle finger of the left on the handle. The little finger of the right hand is then wrapped around the middle finger of the left, and the forefinger of the left is laid against the fingers of the right. Again, fiddle around with this until it feels comfortable. The purpose here is to get the two hands even closer together, allowing them to act more as one during the stroke.

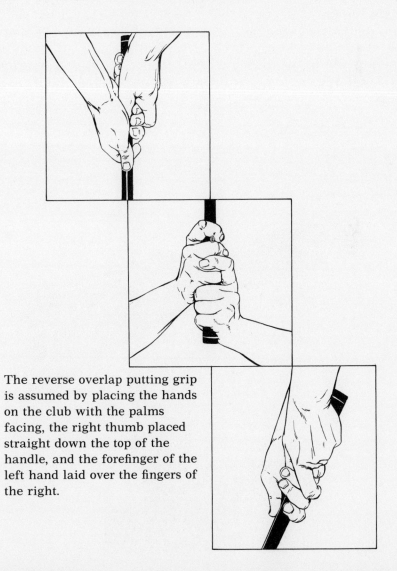

The reverse overlap putting grip is assumed by placing the hands on the club with the palms facing, the right thumb placed straight down the top of the handle, and the forefinger of the left hand laid over the fingers of the right.

With this grip position, we have flared the two hands or put them in opposition to each other. On the normal full shot or pitch shot, the idea is to have the hands working in unison with a cohesiveness that gives you the fullest possible hinging of the wrists on the backswing and an unhinging combined with a rotation of the hands and forearms that gives you the "release" through impact that creates clubhead speed. When you putt, however, you don't want or need that release. You want *stability* that will keep the putterhead square, eliminating any wavering of the toe or heel, and on the correct path during the stroke. In effect, this grip helps restrict the hinging of the wrists during the stroke. Note that I said *restrict* rather than *eliminate.* You want some hinging on the longer putts, but on the medium-length and short putts the hands and wrists should remain firm. You especially don't want the left hand to break down or hinge inwardly, and the opposing grip helps prevent it from doing so. It also encourages the pendulum-type stroke I advocate and which I'll discuss shortly.

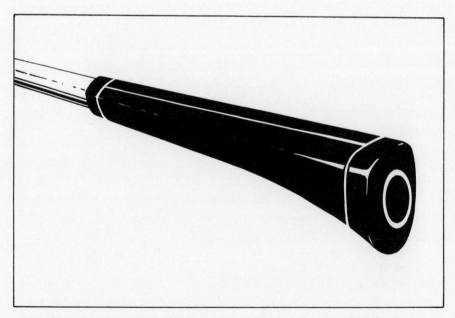

The flat-top, pistol-shaped putter grip lets you put your hands on correctly and more consistently.

The Cross-handed Putting Grip This grip is basically the same as the reverse overlap with one major difference—the left hand is placed below the right. You can crook the little finger of the left hand around the forefinger of the right, lay the right forefinger along the fingers of the left, or any variation that might be comfortable. I've never used the grip, so I guess I can't give you expert advice. Often it is used by players who have had trouble putting with the standard grips, but some very good golfers employ it. Bruce Lietzke, for one, has used it ever since he has been on Tour, and he is one of the top all-time leading money-winners. Bernhard Langer, the 1985 Masters champion, also uses it on the shorter putts with great effectiveness.

The one strong advantage of the grip is that, with the left hand below the right, there is less chance that the right hand will overpower the left and the left wrist will break down, something that ruins a lot of putts with the conventional grip.

Dave Pelz, who has probably made a more thorough study of putting science and technique than anybody I'm aware of, once said that that if we were to start every golfer in the world over again and teach them to putt, without any preconceived notions, the cross-handed method might be the best. We may never know if Dave is right, but if you are having trouble the other way, the cross-handed grip is certainly an alternative to consider.

I said earlier that your feel can change from day to day. That's why I often make adjustments in my putting grip (and everything else, for that matter). For instance, sometimes I overlap the right forefinger over just one finger on the right hand, sometimes over two, which gives me the feeling of putting the two hands closer together. Sometimes I'll flare the hands a little more in opposition, sometimes a little less. It depends on how my hands and my stroke feel on any given day, on how comfortable I am with the putter. That's why at least a short session on the putting green is critical for any player before he starts a round.

However, I do *not* advocate changing things once you start the round. Messing with your grip on every green is only going to ensure that you don't make many putts. Once I've determined what feels best on any given day, I stick with it and so should you.

Now it's vital that you do the same thing every time you put your hands on the club, so I prefer a putter handle that has a flat top and a pistol-type back. It is much easier to put your hands on it in the same place every time because you have that flat top and pistol back as reference points. You can feel more easily where the hands are supposed to be. Especially, you can feel if you have unwittingly made a slight change. Your brain sends you a signal that says, "Wow, I've moved my hands a little bit and it feels funny." With a round grip, you can move your hands a lot and not really notice it.

I'll discuss other factors in putter construction later.

THE GRIP IN BRIEF

- The reverse overlap grip, using either the single or the double overlap, is the most popular for putting. The cross-handed grip also has been effective. Sometimes the regular golf grips—the Vardon and the 10-finger grip—are used for putting.
- Whichever grip you choose, set your hands flared slightly outward, in opposition to each other, to increase stability and reduce excessive hand and wrist motion in the stroke.
- Experiment with the feel and position of your grip in practice, even on the putting green before a round. But once you start to play, put your hands on the putter the same way every time.

Grip Pressure

How you exert pressure when you hold the club is one of the most important considerations in putting and every other aspect of the game.

The key is to keep the pressure constant with all the fingers and the two thumbs. I don't believe in emphasizing pressure in certain fingers over others. Even more important is to keep your grip pressure constant throughout your stroke.

How lightly or tightly you hold the putter doesn't really seem to matter, within reasonable boundaries. Tom Watson has always appeared to hold the putter very firmly. Jack Nicklaus has always appeared to use a light grip. Gary Player has always looked like he is gripping firmly. Bobby Locke, one of history's best putters, always looked like he barely had a hold on the club. So did Bobby Jones, from the films I've seen of him.

Now, don't overdo in either direction. If you hold the putter too tightly, it will create tension that spreads up the forearms and into the shoulders, hindering a fluid stroke. If you hold it too lightly, which really becomes loosely, you will lose control. Somewhere between those two extremes is where you should search for your optimum pressure. I guess I fall somewhere in the middle. My grip pressure is reasonably firm but not so tight that it keeps me from making the smooth, rhythmic stroke I'm after.

But whether your grip is firm or feather-light, it has to stay constant. It can't vary from tight to loose or vice versa during the stroke. Varying grip pressure is the quickest way to lose control and either jerk the putterhead off line or make the face wobble away from square . . . or both.

Experiment to find the pressure that is most comfortable and most effective for you, but once you find it, maintain it throughout the stroke.

GRIP PRESSURE IN BRIEF

- The pressure in all eight fingers and the two thumbs should be the same as you hold the club.
- Do not exert so much pressure that you create tension in the arms and shoulders, and do not hold the putter so lightly that it is loose in your hands. Within this range, your grip pressure can be as firm or light as you prefer.
- Whatever your grip pressure, keep it constant throughout the stroke. Any change will distort the putterhead and the path of your stroke.

The Putter

I don't make any recommendations on the type of putter an individual should use. Whether it is a blade, a mallet, or any variation thereof, whether it is heel-shafted, center-shafted, offset

or whatever, is strictly a matter of personal preference. Whatever
looks and feels good to you, whichever type you can aim better
and, of course, which one works the best for you should be the
determining factors.

I do think the shaft is an extremely important component of a
putter, one that is usually overlooked. The shaft flex in a putter
is as important as the flex in the rest of your clubs. If you like the
way your putter looks but it doesn't feel quite right, you often can
change the shaft and make it feel as good as it looks. When I was
a youngster there was no such thing as a stiff-shafted putter. We
all putted with very flexible shafts, mainly, I think, because the
manufacturers usually took shafts that were too weak for normal
clubs and put them in putters. Now, as shaft technology has ad-
vanced and become more precise, the shaft that isn't strong
enough for a set of clubs is simply discarded. The result is putter-
shafts that, in my opinion, are too stiff for the most part. I pick up
too many putters that seem too stiff, that make it difficult to feel
the ball coming off the face.

I like a puttershaft with some flex in it, one that gives you a
little kick even with a swing that short and slow. I'm sure this
preference goes back to my philosophy that golf is a game of feel.
A more flexible shaft gives me better feel, a softer feel that I like.
You can go too far, of course. If I get a shaft that is too whippy,
I sometimes feel that I can't keep the ball on the green. You may
get the same reaction. You might feel that you are making a good
stroke but the ball is missing the cup left or right. In any event,
if you are having problems with a putter that looks good to you
and the weight feels right, maybe the first thing you should inves-
tigate is the flex of the shaft.

If you had a grip you didn't like, you would change it. With the
help of your professional or a local golf repair shop where the flex
of a shaft can be tested, you can change a shaft about as easily as
you can change a grip.

The weight of your putter again should be your preference and
not anybody else's. And remember here that the weight in the
head also affects the flex of the shaft. If your putter feels light and
stiff, adding some weight to the head also will make the shaft
more flexible.

Some golfers and teachers believe you should change putters

depending on the speed of the greens. I grew up in the south, where the greens were of Bermuda grass and very slow. Everybody said, "The greens are slow so you need a heavier putter." On the other hand, my dad always said that a lighter putter was better on slow greens and a heavier one worked best on fast greens. I suspect he might be right, but I have never changed putters no matter what the speed of the greens. I've always preferred a heavier putter because I think it's better suited to my style of stroke, long and smooth. On slow greens I didn't have to work as hard. The weight of the putterhead encouraged a longer, more flowing stroke. Yet when I began playing the faster bent-grass greens in the north, I enjoyed them very much and was just as effective. I could still make the smooth stroke effectively, and today I am very partial to fast greens.

Around 1975, as I recall, I went to a 38-inch putter, as opposed to the standard length of 35 inches. It was reported that I did this to protect my back, which is partially true, but not because I have a bad back. I'm 6 feet tall and wear a 33-inch sleeve, which means my arms are short for a man of my height. The tips of my fingers might be 2 or 3 inches farther off the ground than those of another 6-footer with more normal arm length. Therefore, I had to bend so low with a 35- or 36-inch putter that it put a tremendous strain on my back. After practicing putting for 15 minutes with a standard-length putter, my back would be killing me. When I went up to 38 inches, I was basically doing the same thing as a man with normal arm length. I was able to stand more erect and ease the strain on my back. And so I could practice longer, for two or three hours at once if I needed to. And anytime you can practice longer, you're going to be better.

By the way, when I increased my putter length to 38 inches, I didn't take any weight off the head, so I added a little overall weight and a lot of swingweight to the club. It's fine for me, because I like to just let the putter swing. Somebody like a Gary Player or an Arnold Palmer, whom I consider jab-type putters, probably would not be as successful with a putter as long and heavy as mine.

So when you are deciding on the length and weight of your putter, take into account your physical dimensions, the type of stroke you prefer, and, most important, what feels good to you.

THE PUTTER IN BRIEF

- Select a putter that looks and feels good to you.
- Choose a puttershaft that is not too stiff, one that gives you some feel when you putt.
- The putter handle should have a flat top and a pistol-type back to help you position your hands more consistently.
- Choose a length and weight that matches your physical dimensions and your type of stroke.

The Setup

Your stance, the way you stand to the ball when putting, involves the position of your feet, the alignment of your body, and the position of your head, all in relation to the ball and the line on which you want to stroke the putt.

In keeping with my overall philosophy, I feel you should stand to a putt in the manner that is most comfortable for you. I have no rigid guidelines on the position of your feet, shoulders, arms, or ears. I have only one opinion about the way you should set up to a putt, and it's a strong one—*position your eyes on a line directly over the ball or just to the inside of it.* Never set your eyes outside the ball and your target line—in other words, past the far side of the ball as you look at it. If your eyes are directly over the ball, it's easy to look directly down the line and sense where you want to direct the putt, so you will make a good stroke. If your eyes are inside the ball, you still get good results because you are "triangulating," looking at the ball from an angle that is compatible with a normal stroke, one that will move inside on the backswing, return to square at impact, and move inside again on the follow-through, just as on a normal full shot. The full swing is a circle, and a putt is just a small portion of that circle.

But if your eyes are outside the ball, you get a distorted view of the line and you tend to take the club away on the outside. So you either have to make some manipulations on the forward stroke—and manipulations are always to be avoided—or you are going to miss the putt left. Everything is out of sync.

I also believe your eyes—your left eye, in this case, if you are a right-hander—should be positioned behind or at least over the ball in relation to the hole. If your eyes are ahead of the ball, you lose the visual relationship between the ball and the hole and again will tend to make a faulty stroke.

Your eyeline also should be straight in relation to the line on which you want your putt to start. If your eyes are crooked, your eyeline set to the left or right of your line, you will tend to stroke the putt in that direction.

The position of the ball in your stance, in relation to your feet, is important in determining its relationship to your eyes. You don't find too many good putters who play the ball far forward, past the toe of the left foot. Then you have a tendency to strike the ball on the upswing or even move your upper body. Subconsciously, I guess, you feel you have to "chase" it when it's that far forward. You also don't see many, if any, good putters who position the ball far back in their stance. This creates a tendency to chop down with the stroke. It also usually gets the ball behind the eyes, which can be fatal.

Most good putters position the ball where, if you would draw a line back on the perpendicular from the target line, it would be somewhere between the left instep and heel. This position would depend somewhat on the width of the stance, of course, but in general it would satisfy all the requirements for correct eye position.

If I had to pick a model setup for putting, it would be that of George Archer or Bob Charles. Both stand with everything—feet, knees, hips, and shoulders—absolutely square. Each puts the ball just forward of middle in the stance, the eyes are correctly positioned, the arms hang nicely. Then the putter just moves back and through. As a result, they are two of the best putters who ever played the game. Ben Crenshaw comes very close to that model and he looks relaxed doing it, and I suspect he's the best putter around today.

When they were kids, someone probably told them, "Look, here is the way you do it—get everything square and level and just hit it." They've become comfortable with that method over the years.

I can't get that precise with my setup. If I try to—and I have tried a hundred thousand times—it feels manufactured and rigid to me. I'm not comfortable. In general, though, I *am* square to slightly open. My feet are 8 or 10 inches apart (measured from the insides of the heels) and are set reasonably parallel to the target line. My weight is set about 60–40 toward my left side and stays there throughout the stroke. If I balanced it 50–50, I might want to start shifting my weight during the swing. My left foot may be pulled back just a little, which sets me slightly open. My shoulders are pretty much parallel to the target line, my upper body is bent comfortably from the hips (but not a lot, thanks to my 38-inch putter), and my arms are hanging freely. But I'll move my feet a little from one day to the next, maybe from one putt to the next, depending on the type of putt it is. My shoulders might open or close a little. I just do what feels comfortable within the basic parameters, always with regard to that correct eye position. No contortions, mind you, just some slight adjustments. Somewhere around square is usually best.

In general, the good putters are those who look good putting. I've had people say to me, "You looked like you were going to make it. You had an air of confidence." To me, that means I was comfortable over the putt and looked like I was.

Having said that, I look at Jack Nicklaus, who crouches, hunches, sets his feet and shoulders open, and looks terribly uncomfortable with his putting setup. But I'm sure he's not, and he also may have been, in his prime, the best putter ever. Certainly he was the best putter under pressure. You see what I mean when I say golf is an individual game. That's why I never say never . . . or always.

THE SETUP IN BRIEF

- Position your eyes on or inside your target line, your left eye above or behind the ball in relation to the target and your eyeline straight with the target line.
- Be comfortable with your setup; ideally, your feet and body parts should be aligned square with the target line, your arms hanging naturally, but it is most important to be comfortable over the ball.
- In general, the ball should be positioned somewhere opposite a spot between your left instep and left heel; playing it forward of the left toe or back of the middle of your stance is not recommended.

The Stroke

Through the years, there have been many good—even great—putters with unorthodox strokes. At least they looked unorthodox by accepted standards. Bobby Locke may have been the finest

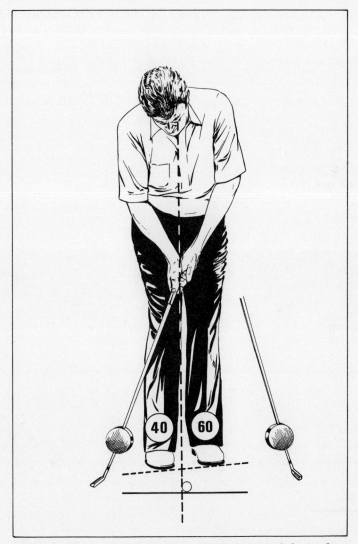

The putting stroke is like the swing of a pendulum, the hands, arms, and shoulders moving together.

putter with the worst action in history. He had a big, broad stroke, aiming way right, bringing the putter way inside and literally hooking the putt, if that's possible. At least it looked as if he did. But no matter what he looked like, he made an awful lot of putts, including a lot of long ones.

The best putter I have ever seen with a peculiar stroke is Billy Casper. At least his stroke is less than classic. He putts basically with his hands and wrists, picking the putter up with a shut face and just laying it back on the ball. But his method has been effective for a long time. He is one of the best ever.

Gary Player has been an effective jab putter, sometimes stab-

The Stroke Is Low and Slow Going Back. On a 20-foot putt, shown here from the face-on angle, the ball is played approximately in the middle of the stance (it looks back here, but only because my stance is slightly open). The stroke is still with the hands, arms, and shoulders, and the putterhead is taken back low and slow. The length of the putt dictates the length of the stroke. The forward swing should accelerate smoothly.

bing the putter into the ground after he makes contact. Gary also has not been afraid to experiment with his putting stroke. He has used a sweeping, pendulum stroke at times. Arnold Palmer has been a wristy putter, and in his prime he was as good as there has been.

The point again is that there are many different ways to do it. Nowadays, we see more of the sweeping, pendulum motion, with little independent action of the hands, than anything else. I'm sure one of the reasons for this is that greens today are uniformly truer and much faster than when golfers like Casper, Palmer, and Player began their careers. Players can *stroke* the putts with a smooth motion rather than *hit* them, which was required on slower greens.

As I have said, I prefer the pendulum-type stroke, and that's what I'll describe to you here. It will be up to you to come up with variations, if any, that best fit your style, ability, and preference.

Putter Stays on Line for the Short Putt. For a putt this short, the
hands, arms, and shoulders move as a unit in the pendulum stroke,
and the putterhead doesn't leave the line, simply moving back and
through to the target.

Please note that I emphasize *type*. A pure pendulum stroke
would have nothing moving but the shoulders, and I think that's
a difficult stroke with which to maintain a good and constant feel.
Basically, it robs you of the feel, the touch, that I try to incorporate
into my stroke. With me, the stroke starts with the shoulders, but
I also move some arms and hands, more or less, depending on the
length of the putt and the swing. It is not a rigid stroke but rather
one in which I try to produce a fluid, rhythmic feel.

To repeat, I feel that the shoulders start my stroke. But because
my hands and arms *are* relaxed rather than rigid, the arms will
swing a little independently of the shoulders and the wrists will
hinge a little bit going back and a little bit coming through. It isn't
a wristy sort of thing. It's simply a natural movement.

The hands work together during the stroke. I feel neither the
left nor the right. Golf is played with both hands, from the putt
to the drive.

My thought is to take the putter back low and slow to the length required for the putt, then gradually accelerate the putterhead through the ball on the forward stroke. That's another reason I call it a pendulum-*type* stroke. A true pendulum swings at the same rate of speed in both directions, but I feel the putter must be accelerating a bit through the ball. This helps keep both the stroke and the ball on line. It's not a *hit,* mind you. It's not a jerk. The acceleration is not rapid. The feeling should be one of smoothness and rhythm in both directions, slow going back and gradually gaining velocity going forward. Because of this acceleration, *the follow-through should be slightly longer than the backswing.*

The distance you roll the putt on the green is determined simply by the length of your backswing. As the length of the putt increases, your stroke gets longer. The pace and rhythm of the stroke should remain the same. On a short putt there will be very little if any hinging of the wrists. Your wrists will hinge more on a longer putt, of course, and your hands will feel more active in the impact area. This is natural, so don't try to stifle it. The key is, whether the putt is long or short, to just *let the putter swing.*

No matter the length of the putt, be it 10 feet or 100 feet, I don't change my grip pressure. The only time I change is on an ex-

tremely fast downhill putt. Then I will lighten the pressure on the
club. Other than that, it stays the same for every putt, and I would
recommend the same for you.

The path of the stroke on a short putt should be basically
straight back and straight through, the blade staying essentially
square to the imaginary target line. But as the putt gets longer, the
putterhead will tend to swing slightly to the inside of that line.
Then it will swing back on line through impact and slightly back
to the inside again on the follow-through.

How much inside the putterhead swings going back and coming through depends, of course, on the length of the putt and also
on the position of your eyes. For example, a player like Fuzzy
Zoeller, who has his eyes set well inside the ball at address, will
tend to swing the club more inside. A player whose eyes are more
directly over the ball will have a stroke that adheres more closely
to the line.

The blade will *appear* to fan open or rotate clockwise on the
backswing, rotating back the other way on the forward swing. It
is really not rotating or twisting. It is simply staying square to the
arc of your swing.

Remember—and I can't emphasize this too strongly—you are
not *making* any of this happen. You are only swinging the putter
within the guidelines of the pendulum-type swing. The putterhead swings inside and the blade rotates only because your shoulders turn and your arms rotate naturally as the swing gets bigger.
In no way should you try to manipulate the putter with your
hands. Just feel you are swinging back and through, keeping everything square.

In this regard, however, do not make an effort to keep the blade
square to the line . . . in other words, as a Ferris wheel would turn.
That would be manipulating, too. Set up correctly with your eyes
in the proper position and just swing your shoulders, arms, and
hands as a unit. Everything else will take care of itself.

It's important to *start* the putterhead straight back. I play in
pro-ams nearly every week, and I see a lot of my amateur partners
having trouble pushing and pulling their putts. This is usually
caused by starting the club back incorrectly. If you start the putter
back and up on the outside of the line, you undoubtedly will return it across the line to the inside and will pull the putt to the left.
If you start the putter back too sharply to the inside, you will

On the Longer Putts, Swing Inside to Inside. As the putts get longer—this one is about 10 feet—the stroke must get longer and the clubhead will swing naturally to the inside of the target on the backswing, returning to the line and then swinging inside again on the follow-through.

swing it back to the outside and will push the putt to the right. So
start it straight back and let the other good things happen naturally.

THE STROKE IN BRIEF

- There are many effective strokes, but the most common
  today is a sweeping, pendulum-type motion; the shoulders,
  arms, and hands move as a unit, but they are not rigid.
  There will be some natural movement of the arms and
  hinging of the hands, especially in the longer strokes.
- The stroke is made with both hands, neither dominating.
- The backswing should be low and slow; on the forward
  swing, smoothly accelerate the putterhead through the
  ball; your follow-through should be slightly longer than
  your backswing.
- The distance the ball rolls is determined by the length of
  your backswing.
- On a short putt, the putterhead swings basically back and
  through on the target line; as the stroke gets longer, it
  starts straight back, then gradually swings inside the line;
  coming forward, it returns to the line in the impact zone,
  then swings gradually inside again on the follow-through.
- The putterface will appear to fan open on the longer
  strokes; actually, it is remaining square to the arc; make no
  independent manipulation with the hands; just let the putter swing.

HOW TO MAKE A PUTT

Armed with the fundamentals, which you have tailored to your
own preferences and hopefully have ingrained with a lot of practice on the putting green, you are ready to put them to use. Now
you must understand that there is a lot more to being a good putter
than just having a good stroke. You have to make that stroke work
where it counts, where all the slopes and speed are different,

where there is pressure and the tournament or the $2 Nassau bet is on the line. Often the good practice putter is a basket case on the course because he doesn't have the proper mental approach, he can't read greens, or he doesn't have a consistent routine. All these elements are critical in achieving what we want, which is making putts.

In this section, then, I'll deal with everything that happens before you pull the trigger and start the putt on its way. If you haven't done all those things correctly, it is unlikely that the putt will find the hole.

The Routine

Every good golfer follows a certain routine on every shot, and this routine is especially important in putting. It is possibly the most important factor in being a good putter. I see many amateurs who step up to a putt one way one time, another way the next time, and I know they have very little chance of being consistent putters. You must be repetitive. Every putt must be approached in the same manner. It doesn't matter what your individual routine is, but you must follow it every time.

Bert Yancey, who has made as thorough a study of the golf swing as anyone, is especially emphatic about the value of a precise routine. He says it eliminates "that awful moment when you must start the swing." I'm sure anybody who has ever played golf understands what he means.

Let me go through my routine for you. I'll discuss some aspects of it more thoroughly later, because the routine is an integral part of everything we do, physically and mentally, as we go about the business of trying to make a putt.

My routine starts when I get the ball back from my caddie after he has cleaned it. I squat and replace the ball in front of my marker, placing the manufacturer's label and the number to the back, where I want to make contact. I walk back and study my intended line. Then I walk forward to the side of the ball and set my putter down behind it, aiming the face down the line I have chosen. I next position my body, probably wiggling my feet a little bit as I get comfortable, aligning myself with the putterface. Do *not* set your body first and then aim the putter. Your aim is likely to be off, somehow you are going to feel uncomfortable, and the putt likely will be ruined before you start.

As I'm getting my body into position, I usually look down my intended line, getting a feel for the speed of the putt and the force I will need in my stroke. I look back down at the ball, focusing on the number on the back. I look down the line one more time (remember, when you do this, rotate your head and keep your eyeline parallel to your target line rather than lifting your head and skewing your eyes). Then I look back at the number, where I want to make contact, and start my stroke.

Simplistically, that is my routine. Those are guidelines. You can find the routine that works for you. Maybe you will incorporate a practice stroke or two. Maybe you will take one look or three or four looks. Whatever you choose to do, ingrain it into your system so you do the same things the same way every time.

THE ROUTINE IN BRIEF

- Establish your own routine, but make sure it is the same on every putt.
- Aim the putterface first; then align your body in relation to it.
- Once you are set over the ball and are confident of the line, trust your routine and go.

Reading Greens

Having replaced your ball, it's time to line up the putt. Hopefully you have done a lot of that, unobtrusively and without bothering any of your fellow players, before it is your turn.

This is an appropriate place to inject a comment or two on pace of play. It has become, in some cases and places, unbearably slow, and much of this slow play takes place on the green. My fellow professionals are often to blame. Some of them take an astounding amount of time lining up their putts. Fans watching on television, especially the kids, see this and figure it's all right for them, too. Well, it isn't, for either the professional or the amateur.

On a putt where I am reasonably sure of the line, I will look at it from only one side, from behind the ball. I don't think it's always, or even often, necessary to look at a putt from more than one angle. You might want to make sure of the slope, up or down, on which the putt will roll, so check the putt from the side. But you can almost always do that discreetly while others are putting or while you are walking up to mark your ball.

On a very important putt for a lot of money and on an unfamiliar course, when I don't want to make a mistake, I may go to the other side of the hole. But I'm talking about tournament conditions here, not everyday play. Checking every putt from all angles can increase your playing time a great deal over the course of a round.

Besides, you often end up confusing yourself. I don't know how many times in my career I've missed putts by looking at them from the other side of the hole. There is almost always a different look to the line from above and below the hole. Now I've put an uncertainty into my mind. Now I make a compromise on the amount of break I want to play. Now I almost always miss and say, "Damn, why did I do that?"

As it turns out, your first look is generally your best one. Just go ahead and trust it. This rule is especially apt for most amateurs, who play one golf course most of the time. When I'm at home and playing Indian Creek, where I live in Miami, I rarely look at a putt from more than one side. I know the greens. If you don't know how most of the putts break on your home course, you haven't been paying attention.

Incidentally, I warn you about watching somebody else putting first on the line of your putt. There are too many variables involved. You never know how hard he hit the putt or even what kind of spin he might have put on it with his stroke. I've seen a player putt a ball that breaks 5 inches. Then I putt right behind him on the same line and the ball doesn't move. So do your own reading; then go with it.

What should you be looking for when you read a green? Basically, three things: slope, speed, and grain. Let's look first at slope, and that's what you have to do—look at it. Then practice on it. First of all, we know the golf ball is round and is going to be influenced by slope. Now we go back to the business of experience and feedback. The only way I know to get a feel for putting on the slant is to practice doing it. Find the slopes on your practice green and stroke putts—right to left, left to right, even up and down. Practice on gentle slopes and sharp ones. If your putting green is relatively flat, as a lot of them are, go out on the course and play a few holes in the evening, taking some extra putts to learn how the ball breaks. (Be sure not to hold up anybody behind you, of course.)

My experience has been that most amateurs, and even a lot of professionals, underread the break of a putt. Almost every breaking putt I see missed is missed on the low side. Players never read enough break because they never think of the ball dying at the hole. They don't consider how much the break will be accentuated as the ball slows down.

I once played a practice round with Bobby Locke before the British Open at St. Andrews, and he said to me, "Laddie, just look around the hole. That's the important spot." What he meant was that you should examine the slope near the cup and visualize how much a slowly rolling ball is going to curve at that point. Depending on the length of the putt and the speed with which you have to stroke it, the slope at the beginning of the putt will not have nearly as much influence, because the ball is traveling faster. If you hit it hard enough, you can keep a putt straight on a vertical wall until it starts to lose speed.

Too many players look at a putt and say, "Aim it an inch left." Then they hit it. This attitude assumes that the putt is going to travel at basically the same speed all the way. And it can be effective on a slow green, especially on the coarser Bermuda grass, because if you miss, the ball is only going to go a foot or so past the hole. On a fast green the ball is going to break much more sharply as it dies or, if you jam the putt, it may go 10 feet past if you miss. Therefore, I would much rather visualize the path that a slowly rolling putt is going to take, see it breaking and dying into the cup.

Your thought should be the same—envision the point at which the ball starts to lose speed and how much the slope is going to grab it at that point. You can practice, too, by stroking easy 4- and 5-footers on the putting green.

As a safeguard, especially if you have any doubt at all about how much the putt is going to break, aim the putt a little higher than you think you should. As long as the ball is above the cup

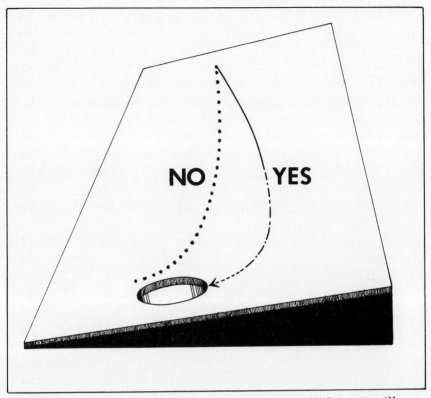

Always play a sloping putt high enough—as the ball slows, it will break more but still have a chance to fall in the hole.

when it starts to die, it still has a chance to go in. It also has more of the cup to catch if it is coming in high and from the side, rather than from the front and low.

Here's a tip that should help you keep the ball up on the slope. On a left-to-right breaking putt I will open my stance slightly, setting more to the left. At the same time I will stand a bit closer to the ball so I don't have to reach for it, especially if the slope is severe. On a right-to-left breaker I will do the opposite, setting more to the right by closing my stance a little and standing slightly farther away so I don't feel crowded. In each case I am predisposing myself to hit the putt a little more up the hill.

For shorter putts with hard, fast breaks I will make a further adjustment. On a right-to-left putt I will play the ball off the toe of the putter; on a left-to-right putt I will play it off the heel. In effect, this technique causes the club to torque or twist a little at impact, but it torques in the correct direction. Playing the ball off the toe causes it to start a little more to the right, and playing it off the heel causes it to start a little more to the left. In each case, you get a little more help in keeping the ball above the hole. Experiment with these variations to better cope with the slick side-hillers.

Which brings us to speed and the fact that speed and slope are closely tied together. We know that a putt on a slope will break more on a green surface that is fast than on one that is slow. If you don't know that instinctively, then you quickly learn it the first time you try a putt.

But *how much* that putt will break, how hard or how soft you

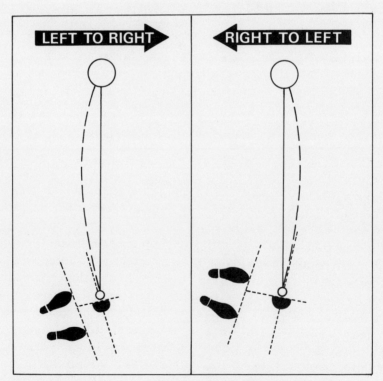

For left-to-right putts, open the stance slightly *(left);* for right-to-left breakers, close it a little *(right).*

On left-to-right putts, position the ball at the heel of the putter *(left);* if the putt breaks right to left, on the toe *(right).*

have to stroke a putt to accommodate the speed of the green, again is a matter of practice. You have to get the information stored in the computer, and the only way you can is to stroke as many putts as you can under the different conditions.

For example, if you normally putt on slow greens and suddenly find yourself on very fast ones, you're in trouble. It is almost impossible to gear down. I have a very close friend who is a member at Augusta National. Once he took three guests there who had never played on extremely fast greens, and the results were hilarious. They were literally putting off the greens. They had no experience to draw on. While they knew the greens were like lightning, their bodies were too used to hitting putts hard and could not adjust in time.

Actually, I think it's more difficult to go from fast to slow greens. It might not be as dangerous, because you might not three-

putt as much, but you won't make many putts. You know you have
to hit the ball harder but somehow your body won't allow you to
do it, so you come up short all the time.

So the best advice I can give if you are going to a course where
the speed of the greens might be drastically different than you are
used to is to skip the practice tee and head right to the putting
green before the round. Stroke as many putts as you can from
different distances. Especially hit a lot of long putts, because they
require the most feel for the speed of the green. The closer you get
to the hole, the more you can eliminate break and try to jam the
ball into the cup. But if you are 60 feet away, you have to get the
ball close enough to have a chance. So the putting practice will
pay off a lot more than hitting a few 8-irons and drivers.

One aspect of the speed/slope combination that is often overlooked is the "up and down" factor. How many times have you
seen a player with a downhill putt on a slick green run the ball

As you approach the green, note how it is set into the
surrounding terrain; this is especially important in the
mountains.

10 feet past the hole, then come up short on the return putt? Many times, I'll bet. He has failed to adjust to the slope, or has failed to realize how much the slope affects speed from the different directions.

The first thing to do here, as soon as you walk onto the green, is to check the line of your putt from the side to determine how much slope there really is. Check quickly and stay out of the way of the other players, of course. Then program your mind to the fact that you are going to have to hit an uphill putt harder than the downhiller. I don't know what the mathematical ratio is, but if the slope is at all severe you're going to have to touch it going down and bang it going up. Here again, practice in those situations whenever you can to get more information into the memory bank.

Finally, if you have trouble determining which way the slope runs and which way the ball will break—and who doesn't?—here is a thought or two that may help. First, as you walk (or ride) to the green, check the surrounding terrain in relation to the putting surface. Sometimes the architect tries to fool us, but the green generally will break in the direction of the land on which it sits.

Playing in the mountains can be particularly deceptive. In general, the putt almost always will break away from the nearest mountain, even when it looks like it will roll in the opposite direction. That's because, appearances to the contrary, the putting surface usually conforms to the overall slope of the terrain.

Greens don't have to be in the Rockies, of course, to be influenced by surroundings. The Upper Course at Baltusrol Golf Club in New Jersey is a good example. It sits at the base of Baltusrol Mountain, which is really nothing more than a big hill. Yet that hill exerts a strong influence on the way a putt breaks. You would swear that putts break uphill on the Upper's greens, but they're really just conforming to the bigger slope.

Another mind game that helps is to imagine a huge bucket of water being poured on the green and visualize where the water will run off. Every well-designed green has to have points where the water drains off the putting surface. If you can determine where these points are for the various portions of the green, you also will learn which way the putts are going to break. Experience and practice—plus keeping your mind awake and your eyes open—can help you a lot in determining slope.

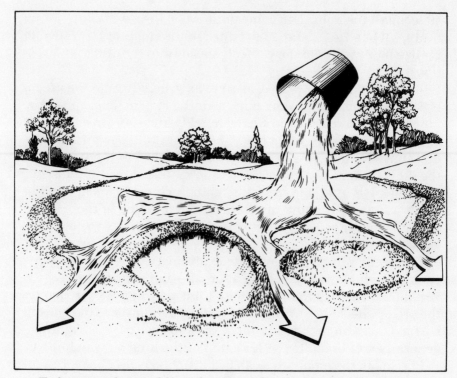

To better understand how the green slopes, envision the various places where water would run off.

Which brings us to grain, the way the grass grows on a green. Grass never grows straight up, which means there is grain in every green, no matter what the course superintendent might say. Grain will have a varying effect on a putt, depending on the length and coarseness of the grass. The longer and coarser the grass, the more effect it will have. On a bent green cut to championship speed, the green will have very little effect, but most of you don't play on that kind of green very often.

How does grain affect a putt? Quite simply, a putt traveling downgrain will roll faster and farther. A putt going upgrain will travel slower and not as far. If the grain is running across your line of putt, the ball will break *more* in the direction that the grain is running and *less* in the other direction. In other words, if the grain is running from right to left, a break to the left will be accentuated and a break to the right will be minimized.

How do you tell which way the grain is running? First, be aware that the bent grasses will grow in the direction of the slope, the way the water runs off the green. Bermuda grasses, usually found in the south and warmer areas, tend to grow toward the setting sun.

Color is an excellent tool in determining the direction of grain. When you look downgrain, the putting surface will appear lighter and have a sheen to it. Looking upgrain, the appearance will be darker and coarser. Stand in the middle of a green and slowly turn in a circle. You will quickly see the difference and be able to figure out how the grass is growing.

On the putting green or in an informal round, you can drag your putter or your hand on the green to check your reading. If

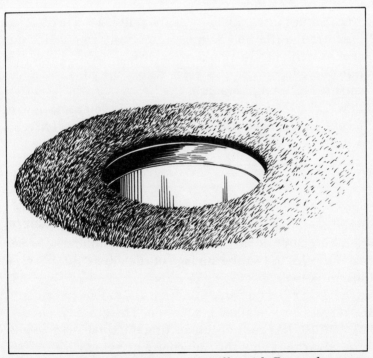

One way to determine grain, especially with Bermuda grass, is to inspect the cup; the grain runs toward the clean-cut side, away from the frayed edge.

READING GREENS IN BRIEF

- As you approach the green, determine the slope of the surrounding terrain; the green usually will slope in the same general direction.
- Envision water being poured over the green and visualize where it will run off; the putts will break in those directions.
- Check grain by looking for color—a light sheen downgrain, darker and coarser upgrain; look around the cup, or examine spike marks. Remember that bent grass grows with the slope or the way the water runs off, whereas Bermuda grass usually grows toward the setting sun.
- Usually look at a putt only from behind the ball, especially on your home course; your first impression is almost always your best one.
- Slope comes into play more as the putt begins to die, so the area around the hole is most important. Don't pick out a spot at which to hit the putt, but visualize the ball dying into the cup. Most putts miss below the hole. Be sure to start the ball high enough.
- Practice to learn how speed and slope interact, how different green speeds affect the amount a ball will break on a hill.

---

you drag the putter upgrain, the grass will kick up. Downgrain it will not. You can't do any of this in a real round, of course. It is against the rules to test the surface of the green. But it's effective as a learning tool.

One trick I've learned over the years is to look at spike marks where players have walked before you. The grass, of course, will pull up against the grain. By inspecting the spike marks carefully you can tell which way the blades are growing.

You also can look at the cup to determine which way the grain runs. The side from which the grain is running will have grass on it, sometimes growing over the lip late in the day. On the opposite side, the grass will be worn off, because the cup-cutter has cut off the roots of the blades. Early in the morning, when the cup is fresh, this doesn't work very well. But later in the day, when the grass has grown, it's an excellent method.

Grass, of course, does grow, and it's something to be aware of, especially if you are playing later in the day. It grows especially fast in the warmer climates. Consequently, the greens will get slower as the day goes on. At Indian Creek, where I live, we try to cut our greens to a speed of 8½ feet on the Stimpmeter, which is an instrument for measuring green speed by determining how far the ball rolls. Right after the greens have been mowed in the morning and the grass has dried, they measure 8½ feet. By 4:30 in the afternoon they have slowed down to 7 or 7½ feet. You may seldom have to take this factor into account, but if you are playing more than one round in your club tournament or the member-guest, you must consider it. The last putt of the day will be slower than the first one.

The Yips: Cause and Cure

This is one of my favorite topics, because at one time or another the yips affect everyone who plays golf—you, me, the best putters in history. The subject, the cause and the cure of the yips, certainly ties in with the following section, but because it is such an ever-present phenomenon, and because I think I have the solution to it, I will deal with it separately.

The yips are simply a case of bad strokes, usually on short putts. They show up in many forms, but the sum of it is that you simply can't get the short putts in the hole. Quite often a player with the yips can make smooth strokes on 30-footers and make his share of them. But from 5 feet in he's a basket case.

History is full of famous victims: Sam Snead, Ben Hogan, Arnold Palmer, Jack Nicklaus, even Tom Watson to an extent. They may not all qualify as full-fledged yippers, but certainly they don't make putts the way they did when they were winning everything in sight.

The popular explanation for the yips is that the nerves go, that the wear and tear of competitive pressure over the years frazzles the nervous system. In one respect that's true, but I contend that the problem is not physical. The yips are not caused by shaky hands but instead by shaky emotions. I've known 25-year-old amateurs who could not make a 1-foot putt. The problem is anxiety. It's a psychological hang-up. That's why the yips show up on the close-range putts. They're the ones you know you should make. Once you miss a few, the fear builds. The fear feeds on itself, and soon you have a full-blown case of the yips.

Snead is probably the best example. He was always one of the best long putters in the game, and he was a pretty good short putter, too. He had a reputation for missing the short ones, stemming mostly from the 39-incher he missed to lose the 1947 U.S. Open to Lew Worsham, but he pooh-poohs that. "I missed a lot of short ones," he once said, "because I had more chances to miss them than anybody else."

Eventually, however, Snead began to miss so many short ones that he abandoned the conventional style of putting and switched, first to the croquet style that was quickly outlawed and then to the sidesaddle method that he made famous. With that, he could putt acceptably if not brilliantly. Yet—and this makes my point—I've seen Snead on the practice green putting conventionally, stroking the ball smoothly and making putts. And he admits that he can do it at practice but not on the course when the pressure is on. It's not a physical problem; it's a mental one.

I could go on and on with examples. I think the long putter that is currently in vogue with so many players on the Senior Tour is a concession to psychological problems rather than physical ability. Orville Moody, who was never a good putter when he played on the regular Tour, has made a handsome living since he went to the long putter. But I think this case is a matter of a new mental approach rather than a better method. Having gone to a new style, he now thinks he can make putts, so he does.

I've had the yips. I've gone through periods in which I got so uptight on short putts that I was making strokes so bad you couldn't believe them. Certainly I couldn't believe them. I'm sure you've had similar bad times.

I don't know how you got rid of them, if you have. Obviously some players never do. But I know how I conquer them whenever they crop up. I figured out that a yip is simply a movement. You become so apprehensive on a short putt, you want so badly for it to go in the hole, that you look at the hole to make sure it goes in before you make contact with the ball. Your eyes move and your head moves.

Moving the head is not as much a problem as what it causes. When you move your head, your shoulder moves, usually flaring to the left. If it were a full swing, we would call that "coming over the top." That's basically what you are doing on a putt. So you either pull the ball to the left or you instinctively counter with your hands and push it to the right. Either of these we call "quit" strokes. You don't make a smooth, accelerating movement of the putter toward the hole. And you miss the putt, and the next one, and the next one, and pretty soon you're so befuddled you don't have a chance.

The cure is simple—keep your head and eyes still. How do you do that? Remember when I suggested that when you replace your ball you position the number at the back, at the point where you want to make contact? Do this and now simply look at it. Keep your eyes focused on that spot as if it were a tack that you are

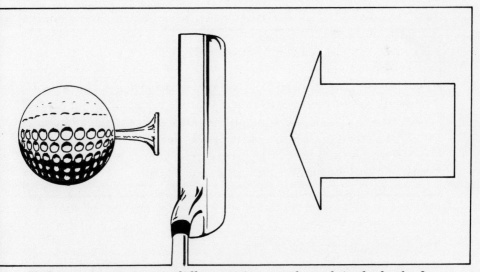

To hit your putts more solidly, envision a tack stuck in the back of the ball and strike that tack with the center of your putterface.

going to hit with a hammer. The face of your putter is the hammer. Get the face aimed down your target line; then watch the blade drive that little tack into the ball. Don't focus on the ball in general. Zero in on that spot and keep the picture clear. If you move your eyes and your head, the picture will blur. Don't worry about where the ball is going. Just see the hammer hit the tack. If you keep your eyes steady, everything else will stay steady, and suddenly those little putts will start falling. Soon your apprehension will disappear and the yips will be gone.

There is a more sophisticated method that accomplishes the same thing if you want to try it. Aim the putter at the hole; then look at the hole and, while still looking at the hole, make your stroke. Now you are already looking at the target, so you are not going to move. A pool player does the same thing, so we're not breaking new ground here.

I would not recommend that you do this during a round without first practicing it, but it does work. Johnny Miller won the 1987 AT&T tournament with this method, and Danny Edwards used it successfully for a while on Tour. It simply does the same thing as my antidote. It keeps you from moving on the putt.

However you do it, stay steady and say good-bye to the yips.

THE YIPS IN BRIEF

- The yips are caused by anxiety, which causes the eyes, head, and shoulders to move.
- Cure the yips by focusing on the number at the back of the ball and swinging the putterhead into that number, as if driving a tack with a hammer; that keeps your eyes and head still and the putts will start to fall.

The Essence of Putting

Given all this knowledge that you now have assembled, you are still faced with performing the most important act in golf. You have the grip, the setup, the stroke, and the routine. You have read the green and have a good idea of the break. Now you have to make the putt.

Here is where you must let your senses take over, where you must give in to feeling and to positive thoughts. The essence of putting, as with any other successful shot in golf, a successful play in any other sport, or any success in life, is that you believe you can do it and don't get in your own way.

Don't get in your own way—what does that mean? Essentially it means don't interfere with the natural processes that you have ingrained through practice and experience. Visualize and feel what you have to do; don't let negative thoughts intrude; then go ahead and do it. Trust that it is going to happen.

The first thing you must do is see the line. This procedure doesn't have to be a mathematical computation. In fact, it shouldn't be. You know all about slope and speed and grain at this point. Now just relax and let the visualization process work. Literally try to see the line of the putt. Imagine the ball rolling up the slope and curling into the hole. *Always* see it falling into the hole. I strongly believe you can will a putt into the hole (just as you can, by negative thinking, will it *out* of the hole).

There is not a better putter on Tour today than Ben Crenshaw. He has a marvelous stroke, of course, but he has more than that. He has the confidence that he is going to make a good pass at the ball, he has the imagination to see the line of the putt, and he has the intelligence not to do anything to screw it up.

I've seen Ben make putts that he really doesn't look at in the accepted fashion. He doesn't actually get down and sight them from either side. He just kind of stands there, somewhere behind the ball, and looks, taking in the whole situation and letting his mental processes work. And when he walks into the ball, he is seeing a line. He knows it is going to go on that line, and it does. And it usually goes in.

Crenshaw believes in himself. Even when he misses, his confidence is unshaken. He knows he is human and does not make the perfect read or the perfect stroke every time. He knows that even if the putt is perfect, the green surface is not. There are too many variables to expect to hole every putt. But he will be expecting to make the next one. Crenshaw's attitude is the one I like to take into every putt, and it should be your attitude, too.

You will rarely make a putt when you don't think you can, when you don't trust the line or your mechanics, when your approach is negative. Don't stand over a putt and tell yourself that you are aimed too far to the left, or to the right, that it's an uphill putt and you have to be sure to hit it hard enough, that it's a downhill putt and you have to be careful with it. Don't be worrying about the kind of stroke you will make. Those worries are negatives, and they will invariably cause you to miss.

Bruce Crampton was one of our finest players for years, as well as one of our best putters. He is now one of the best on the Senior Tour. Bruce once said, "If you are looking for ways to miss a putt, you will find one." How true. You are trying to make the putt, not miss it, but too many players never give themselves a chance because they stifle the instincts that would let them succeed.

Here is where a solid routine is invaluable. Take a look at the putt, visualize where it is going to go, walk into the ball, set your putter down, and let your internal mechanism take over. Give your senses a chance.

I've had great success with this method. I've had players ask me, after I made a putt that looked particularly difficult, how I played it. And I had to say, "Well, I just kind of felt it. I didn't really play a break, I just got over the putt and *felt* it into the hole."

This holds true for a putt of any length. I hear a lot of talk, especially on television, about "three-putt territory" and "he's just trying to get it close for a two-putt." Well, in truth, nobody makes a lot of long putts, but that's no reason not to try. I've had many 10-footers where, depending on the slope and the speed of the green, I was putting defensively and just hoping to get down in two. On the other hand, when you are facing a 30-footer on a reasonably level green where the putting surface is true, it's not unrealistic to try to hole it. I certainly don't step up to a long putt with the idea of trying to get it close. There is nothing that says, "It's against the law to make a 40-footer, so all you can do is try to two-putt it." Any golf shot, from as far as you can hit the ball to a 1-inch putt, has a chance to go in. So if you can hit it far enough, why not try to make it?

I have made putts longer than 100 feet in tournament play. If I have done it once, I can do it again. Why would I want to give up on the possibility and just try to roll the ball to somewhere within the vicinity. Line it up, visualize it, and try to make it.

I'm not telling you to be foolish, of course, and whack every putt way past the hole just on the chance that it might catch the cup and go in. That kind of putt probably wouldn't go in anyway, even from 10 feet. I'm just telling you to approach a long putt as you would a short one and give yourself a chance to make it.

In 1980, I was a stroke behind Jack Nicklaus going to the seventy-first hole of the Doral-Eastern Open. I hit my second shot to the back of the seventeenth green and was left with about a 60-foot downhill putt on an incredibly fast green. I didn't say, "Oh, my goodness, I hope I can two-putt." That never entered my head. I felt good, I felt comfortable over the ball, I saw a line, and I stroked the putt. The putt leaked down the hill, made a break off the slope—it seemed like it took two minutes to get to the hole—and fell right in the middle. And I went on to win the tournament.

I hit a similar putt on the eighth hole in the third round of the 1986 U.S. Open at Shinnecock. I had been struggling a little and was in danger of falling out of contention. I had played a bad drive into the rough and had just barely gotten the ball on the front edge of the green, about 60 feet away. And the feeling came over me again. I looked down the line and saw the ball going in. I was comfortable over the putt and stroked it. It went down my intended line, took the break I had visualized, and fell in. I have seen that putt on film, and it looks as if I were in a trance. I didn't have a reaction to the putt going in, because I had already seen it go in before I putted it.

Voodoo? No, I think it is more a culmination of all I have talked about in this chapter. I know how to putt, I know how to read greens, I have confidence in myself, and I don't get in my own way. I have the mental discipline to package all this knowledge into a thought process that lets me visualize a putt and then go ahead and let it happen. This discipline comes from years and years of competitive experience. I can't expect you to have that same backlog of information in the computer. But you have some, and you can add to it every day or every week. Then trust it. Let it work.

After all, the worst thing that can happen is that you will miss the putt. And by interfering with your mind and body, by getting in your own way, I'll guarantee that you were going to do that anyway.

Trust yourself and your instincts. In the long run, you will make many more putts than you miss.

Remember, you're a good putter. Don't ever forget it.

THE ESSENCE OF PUTTING IN BRIEF

- Let your senses take over.
- Keep out the negative thoughts; if you look for ways to miss a putt, you will find one.
- Visualize the putt breaking and falling in; "see" the line and "feel" yourself reacting to it; then go through your routine and make your stroke.
- Trust your instincts and your ability; let it happen.

3

PUTT YOUR CHIPS TO MAKE IT EASY

In the 1980 Doral-Eastern Open I was in a playoff with Jack Nicklaus on the par-4, sixteenth, our second extra hole. I put my second shot just over the green on the second cut of fringe. The pin was back and I was only 20 feet away, but there was some grass behind the ball that made the lie a little funny. Nicklaus had a 12-foot putt for birdie, and it looked like I was in trouble.

I took my sand wedge, delofted it a little, and made it into about a 9-iron. I played the ball back slightly in my stance so I could hit down a little more sharply on the back of the ball and overcome the hair behind it. Then I chipped it into the hole.

Nicklaus was so surprised that he missed his putt and I won the tournament.

A sensational shot? Well, under the circumstances I suppose it looked like it. Actually, as far as I was concerned at the moment, it was no more than a 20-foot putt. After I had solved all the problems with some preliminary planning, all I had to do was stroke it.

Chipping is a problem for a lot of amateurs. I see chip shots chili-dipped and left short. I see them bladed far past the hole or over the green. Yet I never see anybody do these things with a putt—I see putts that are long or short, but I can't recall seeing one that was topped or hit fat.

The answer to better chipping, then, is to use the method I use—*chipping is simply putting with a lofted club.*

The Chipping Stroke Is a Putt. The only difference between a chip and a putt is the club you have in your hands. Both are made with the putting grip and a pendulum stroke, the hands, arms, and shoulders moving as a unit. As you can see here, there will be some hinging at the wrists in a longer stroke, but this is simply the result of the length of the stroke and is not consciously done.

A chip is a low shot with a lot of roll, the same as a putt. The only difference is that a chip gets airborne at the start, for a short period of time, to clear the area just off the green. There is no need to create power or great distance in the swing. Accuracy and distance judgment are the critical factors, just as in a putt. So treat it as a putt. It makes everything a lot simpler.

Now, you may ask, if I am in effect putting the ball anyway, why don't I just go ahead and use a putter and remove *all* margin for error? Some good players do. Tom Watson, for example, seldom chips from the edge of the green, using his putter instead. And he holes more of them than I do. But Watson has always been an aggressive putter. He puts more "pop" on the ball than I do and gets it slightly airborne anyway, which helps it get over the irregularities before it reaches the putting surface.

It is the variation in the length and grain of the grass on the fringe and just beyond that I am trying to avoid by using a club with some loft. It is very difficult for me to judge how fast or slow a ball will go through grass that is very high, and you never know for sure when it might be kicked off line or take a couple of hops that change the speed and the distance it will roll. I know there is nothing in the air that will deflect the ball, so I would rather travel by air until I can get the ball onto the smoother putting surface.

I think the reason most people use a putter from off the green instead of a club with loft is that they don't have confidence in their chipping (this is not the case with Watson, I'm sure). But by learning to chip with the putting method, the doubt is erased. You can make the stroke, confident in your ability to make good contact and also assured that there will be no surprises on the way to the green.

The only time I might use a putter from off the green is when I am not sure how hard or soft the putting surface is where I want to land the ball. Then, assuming that the intervening grass is not too high and that it is reasonably smooth, I'll go ahead and roll the ball so it doesn't have to land. But those occasions are rare. The putt with a lofted club is by far my preference.

The fundamentals of grip, setup, and swing are the same as for a putt. If you have assimilated the thoughts I discussed on putting in the previous chapter, you are 90 percent along the way to becoming a good chipper. Chipping is more complex than putting only in the area of club selection. And occasionally you will have to contend with a difficult lie, which is never the case on the green.

Let's quickly review the putting fundamentals that should be applied to chipping:

• Use your putting grip, the reverse overlap, or whatever other grip you have chosen. Grip down on the handle of the longer clubs for more control. Use primarily the same grip pressure as in putting, balanced in both hands, not so tight as to cause tension and not so loose as to lose control of the club.

• Set up as you do for a putt, your stance square or slightly open to the target. Stand reasonably erect, your arms hanging naturally, your weight slightly favoring your left side. Your eyes—and this is just as important here as in putting—should be over or inside the target line, and your eyeline must be straight with the target line.

At this point, you must take into account the length of the club you have in your hand and adjust it to your normal putting setup and, especially, the correct eye position. Your sand wedge and pitching wedge normally are about the length of your putter, so you probably will want to hold them at the end. As the club gets longer, you should grip down on it to, in effect, make it putter-length.

• Use the pendulum-type swing, the same as with your putter; it just gets a little longer as the shots get longer. Make it low and slow going back, and accelerating smoothly coming forward, contacting the ball at the bottom of the stroke with no manipulation. Don't be rigid with it, remembering instead to let a little independent action of the arms and hinging of the hands happen naturally with the longer strokes; the key is to stay still over the ball with your body and your head, keep eye contact with the ball, and swing smoothly.

If you do happen to prefer a wristy putting stroke, one with more independent hand action, go ahead and hit your chip shots the same way.

• Use the same routine that you do in putting, even reading the green and picking out an intended line—after all, this is really just a putt.

* * *

The grip, setup, and pendulum-type stroke may feel awkward if you are used to using your regular playing grip and hitting the chip shot with more hand action. The method I'm recommending will feel a bit stiff for a while, mainly because you are basically taking the hinging of the hands out of the stroke. And that's the idea. Most of the bad chip shots happen because the player gets the hands overactive, usually going too fast, and ruins the stroke.

Because it will feel awkward, *practice* is required—there's that word again. You will particularly have to practice chipping the ball different distances, which seems to be the most difficult aspect of acquiring skill with this method. But you already know the fundamentals and the stroke. It's just a matter of applying them to different clubs and different lies. It won't take long.

Club selection is the critical factor in chipping success. Instead of using just one or two clubs for chipping, as many golfers do, I use as many clubs as are necessary, everything from the 4-iron to the sand wedge, and I recommend you do the same. Use the less-lofted clubs when a foot or two off the putting surface and go all the way up to the sand wedge when several yards away. The idea is to use your chipping stroke, land the ball safely on the green in all cases, and let it roll to the hole. Club selection and length of stroke will vary, then, with your distance from the green, the location of the hole on the putting surface, and the speed of the green.

By meeting the demands of each particular chip shot with a different club selection, you basically avoid having to make adjustments in your swing. Sometimes it will be a little longer, sometimes a little shorter, but even those adjustments are minimized by changing clubs. In other words, the type of shot you are going to hit and the results have been predetermined by the club you have chosen. You have solved most of your shot problems before you ever step up to the ball.

The key, then, is learning how each club performs and, subsequently, how the ball performs. You must learn how far to carry each shot in the air, then how far it will roll under different green and slope conditions.

The rule of thumb in chipping is that the ball should fly as short a distance as possible and roll as far as possible. In other

A Guide to Club Selection. The balls illustrate a general guide to the distances from which I use a 5-iron (closest), 7-iron, 9-iron, and sand wedge for my chip shots. But other variables like firmness and speed of the green and the position of the hole also must be considered in choosing the club.

words, you want as little air time and loft on the shot as you can. The higher and farther it travels, the more possible variance you can get when it lands. You want to keep it as low as possible and land it as quickly as possible, then let it roll to the hole.

This does not mean, however, that you should flirt with the fringe. Don't try to land the ball an inch onto the putting surface. If you miss by an inch and a half, the ball could hang up on you, or at least the eventual distance will be altered. Within the guidelines I just prescribed, give yourself a comfortable margin for error.

Another thought to keep in mind is that you want to make as small and as smooth a swing as possible. The longer the swing, the more "hit" you have to apply, and the more chance there is of mishitting the shot. That's true with every shot and every club, from the putter to the driver. So choose the least-lofted club possible that will send the ball the required distance with the smallest swing.

On the other hand, don't use a club with too little loft for the distance required, so that you feel you have to hit the shot too easily. Remember, there should always be some acceleration on the forward stroke. If you feel you don't have enough loft in your hand, you will tend to quit on the stroke and mishit it.

Remember, also, one of the fundamentals of the putting setup and stroke—keep your head and eyes still during the swing. This rule is especially critical on the longer shots. They will involve swings that are longer than you normally make in putting. Any head movement could ruin the shot.

Here are some examples of how I vary my club selection in

The Longer the Shot, the Longer the Stroke. As the distance a chip must travel to the green gets greater, a more-lofted club must be used and the stroke gets longer. But, as seen in the sequences on pages 87–89, the pendulum action remains the same. Only in the very longest strokes is there any appreciable hinging at the wrists.

different chipping situations. We're going to assume for the moment that the green is reasonably level and of average speed. It's impossible for me to cover every eventuality, of course, but I'll give you some standards. Then, through practice and experience, you will learn to adjust to different shot requirements.

If I am just off the green, on the fringe or just beyond, and the pin is a comfortable distance away—say 25 or 30 feet—I would use a 5- or 6-iron, land the ball on the green, and let it roll to the hole. From 4 or 5 feet farther back, I now have to make a little longer swing to land the ball on the green, so the 5-iron would come off too hot. Now I switch to a 7-iron that gives me added height on the shot so the ball will still roll the same distance. From 8 or 10 feet away, I might have to go to a 9-iron to achieve the same result. If I am 15 feet or so back from the edge of the green, I would probably take out the sand wedge. But I would still employ the same method, using the putting stroke. Even with the sand wedge, I am not *trying* to hit the ball higher. The loft of the club will take care of that.

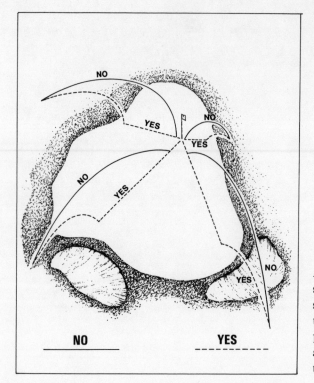

All chip shots should be landed safely as close to the fringe as possible and allowed to roll to the hole.

Now let's go through that same sequence of shots if the cup is 60 or 70 feet from the edge of the green. From the fringe or just behind, I might use a 4-iron and make a slightly longer swing. From 5 feet back I can still probably use a 5-iron. From 10 feet away I could use the 7, from 15 feet the 9. With that much green to work with, I probably could use the sand wedge, still employing my putting stroke, from 25 or 30 feet off the green.

Conversely, if the cup were cut just 12 or 15 feet in, I would have to use a more-lofted club, an 8- or 9-iron, right from the start. The sand wedge with the putting stroke might be effective only from 8 or 10 feet back. After that, I'd have to go a pitch shot and do something funny with it.

You get the idea. Those are the guidelines. Now you must learn to adjust for different conditions. If the green is slower and/or the shot is uphill, you can use a less-lofted club and make a longer swing. If the green is faster and/or downhill, you must use more loft and a smaller swing. Whether the green is wet or dry can make a big difference. As you can see, there can and will be various combinations of those conditions. The only way to learn to cope with them is to practice. The more you do, the better your mind and body will instinctively adjust to the requirements of each shot you face on the course.

As you become more accustomed to the method and more

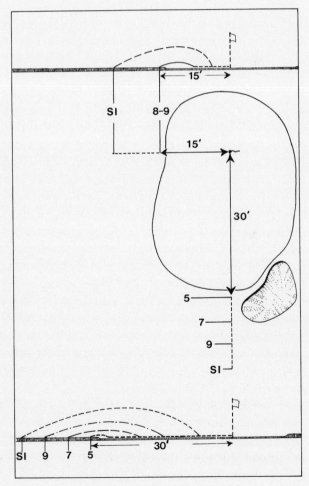

The closer you are to the fringe, the less lofted the club used. As you move farther away, the more-lofted club selected will fly higher and roll less, so it should be landed closer to the hole.

skilled in using it, there are variations you can introduce that will help you handle unusual conditions. For example, on the shot I described at Doral, there was some grass behind the ball. So I set my hands a bit forward, hooding the sand wedge a little and turning it into a 9-iron. Then I picked the club up a little more sharply on the backswing and swung into the ball on a little steeper angle. This got me through the grass and imparted a little spin on the ball to slow it down once it hit the green. You might want to try the same shot, but learn it in practice first.

There are times when you might want to grip a little shorter or a little longer on a particular club, depending on the distance required. For example, on a long chip with a 4-iron when the green is fast, when you don't have to make as big a swing, you might want to grip down for better control. If the green is slow or the shot is longer, you might want to move up on the handle so you can make a more forceful stroke with less effort. It's simply a matter of length giving you more leverage.

You also can adjust the spin on the ball, which affects the distance it will travel. Normally, on a chip shot with a putting stroke, you want to impart as little spin to the ball as possible, in keeping with the philosophy that you make the chip as much like a putt as possible. But sometimes, especially on shots to a close-cut hole, you might want to check the ball while still using the putting method. Simply use the right hand a little more quickly on the forward stroke to slip the clubface under the ball. Don't turn the right hand over; instead, feel that is almost turning *under.* Using the right hand in this manner will increase the clubhead speed and change the angle to impart more backspin.

If the green is slow or the shot is uphill and you want to put less spin on the ball and get it rolling better and farther, do just the opposite. Turn the right hand *over* through impact.

Again, all of these variations require practice before you can use them in actual play. They are really professional-type subtleties. Use them only if you know what you are doing, and even then only when you must.

Your best bet is to stick with the basics. Play the proper shot with the proper club. This rule will help you under pressure, because you are doing what you know best. Only if the lie or other circumstances dictate should you try something different.

* * *

Your strategic approach to chipping should be basically as it is to putting. On a relatively level shot with no extraordinary problems, go ahead and try to make it. But there is a time for caution. Obviously you must be careful on a slick, downhill shot. You also should play defensively on a fast, contoured green where you face a shot that could break sharply and finish far from the cup. In such cases, when you are not trying to hole the shot, leave the pin in and try to make sure the ball finishes below the hole, leaving you an uphill putt that is as short as possible.

I have often been asked how I handle an uphill shot to a two-tiered green when the hole is on the upper tier. If the levels are sharply defined, it is better to pitch the ball to the upper level, provided, of course, that there is plenty of room to land and stop the ball close to the hole. Otherwise you should chip it. In this case, use a lower-lofted club and make sure the ball is rolling before it comes to the slope. If you try to land it into the slope or just short of the slope, it might die or it could hop too far and run well past the hole.

In all cases, you must first visualize the shot, imagining the line and how the ball is going to break. If you can call on past experiences, do so to make the body work to fit the requirements of the shot.

Do you believe in visualization? Do you believe in déjà vu? If not, you had better start, because it does pay off in golf. Let me tell you another story. Remember my chip-in against Nicklaus on the sixteenth hole at Doral in 1980? In 1988 I was again playing with Nicklaus in the final round. My second shot ended up in exactly the same place on the sixteenth hole. The hole was in exactly the same place as it had been in 1980. Nicklaus was standing in the same place. His caddie and my caddie were in the same place. I took the same sand wedge, hooded it the same way . . . and chipped it into the hole. This time it wasn't for the title, but it put me into fourth place alone and was worth several thousand dollars.

It was eerie, déjà vu in a nutshell. But this incident just happened to be at the same place with the same cast of characters. Between 1980 and 1988, I had chipped that same shot into the hole in different tournaments seven or eight times. Every time I was faced with a shot like that, I would instinctively say to myself, "Boy, this is that shot at Doral." And often I would hole it. That's simply using positive feedback. I would subconsciously relate to a positive experience in the past, so I knew I could do it again.

If you are using your mind properly and playing the shot you have practiced, it can work for you, too.

CHIPPING IN BRIEF

- The chip shot is simply a putt with a lofted club.
- Utilize your putting grip, setup, and stroke.
- Practice to become comfortable with the stroke.
- Vary your club selection to fit the shot required. Use less loft from close to the green and more from farther away. Consider the location of the hole, the speed of the green, and the slope; then simply choose the correct club and vary the length of your stroke.
- Be sure you land the ball on the green; don't flirt with the edge of the fringe.
- Visualize—see the line and how the ball will roll, and call on your past experience to make the shot.

4

PITCHING

Toss It High to Get It Close

As we move far enough away from the green that it becomes impractical to use the chipping method, or when there is an intervening hazard that must be carried with a high, soft shot, we must turn to the pitch.

The pitch is simply a miniature version of the full swing. The setup is the same, the arms swing more fully than in the chip shot, and the legs and body come into play. I hit my sand wedge a maximum of 85 yards, so when I am hitting a 50-yard pitch shot I am coming very close to a full swing. So I will begin this chapter with a quick discussion of the fundamentals of that swing. The discussion will include the grip, the posture and alignment, and the swing itself, with an emphasis on how it all should be done for the pitch shot.

THE GRIP

The grips most commonly used for pitching and the rest of the full shots are the Vardon or overlapping grip, the interlocking grip, and the 10-finger grip—actually, eight fingers and two thumbs.

Vardon Grip

Place your left hand against the handle of the club with your wrist high and your fingers extended and pointing down, the handle resting underneath the heel pad and running across the palm to the base joint of your forefinger. The handle should be farther underneath the heel pad than it is in the putting grip.

Now close your fingers around the handle. The club will be secured between the heel pad and fingers, the pad forming a vise that holds the club firmly. Your forefinger should be crooked around the club but not separated from the middle finger. Your thumb should rest on the top of the handle, just slightly to the right side. The V formed by your thumb and forefinger should point generally toward your right shoulder. Again, experiment to determine how "weak" or "strong" you want your grip to be. The grip that is strong or turned more to the right will allow more rotation of the club and clubface through impact, generally—but not always—producing a hook or right-to-left action of the ball. The grip that is weaker or turned more to the left will inhibit rotation. So the position of your hands should be determined by your strength and physical characteristics plus the shape of your shots—or the shape you want them to be.

Often neglected is exactly *where* on the handle the left hand should be placed. The grip cap or butt end of the club should extend just behind the heel pad. Too many players set it against the heel pad, which means they are losing strength and control. I've had amateurs ask me why I choke up on the club. I don't. I put it where it belongs for maximum effectiveness.

The right-hand position should more or less match that of the left. In putting, remember, you want the hands opposed to create stability, but in the rest of the shots you definitely want them working together.

Place the right hand against the side of the shaft with the handle against the roots of the fingers, just under the callous pads. Close the first three fingers around the club, crooking the forefinger slightly. Now simply hook the right little finger around the left forefinger. Ideally it should rest in the groove between the left forefinger and middle finger, hooked around the forefinger. If you set it too much on top of the forefinger, your right hand will tend to ride too high or too much to the left. At this point, your left thumb should be snuggled into the channel between the heel and thumb pads of the right hand. Your right thumb should be resting just to the left of the top of the handle and the V should be pointing in the same direction as the left-hand V. Both Vs should be "closed" at the top rather than gapping.

Your two hands now should feel as if they are snugly together, rather than separated, so they can work as a unit. The palm of the right hand should be pretty much aligned with the back of the left, allowing the two hands to work together. Within these guidelines, experiment with how much left or right you want to set your

These illustrations of the full-swing grip show that the Vs formed by the thumbs and forefingers both point to the right shoulder, the little finger of the right hand is hooked over or around the forefinger of the left, and the club rests under the heel pad of the left hand.

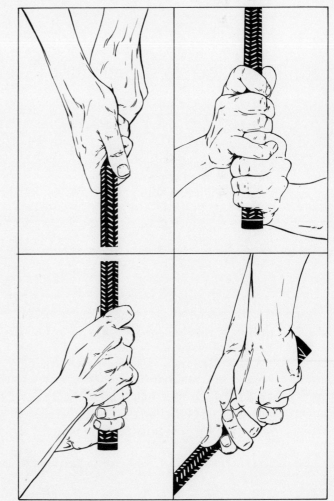

hands on the club and let the results determine what is best for you.

Interlocking Grip

This grip often is used by players with smaller hands—Jack Nicklaus and Tom Kite are perhaps the best-known proponents—although hand size is not necessarily a criterion.

The grip is formed exactly like the Vardon grip with one exception—the little finger of the right hand is hooked *under* the forefinger of the left and rests between the forefinger and middle finger; consequently, the left forefinger is hooked *over* the right little finger. Everything else should look the same.

Setting the hands in a "weaker" position, turned more to the right, helps to keep them from turning over through impact and results in a higher trajectory for the pitch shot.

10-Finger Grip

This grip sometimes is referred to as the "baseball" grip, but the description is inaccurate. The grip is formed and looks the same as the other two grips except that the little finger of the right hand does not overlap or interlock. It is curled around the handle with the rest of its companions, resting snugly against the forefinger of the left.

In effect, the hands are covering more of the handle and the right hand is sitting more toward the head end of the club. This position will tend to make the right hand more active, which is often a benefit for players who have trouble rotating or releasing the clubface through impact.

Is it for you? As I say, experiment and find out.

GRIP PRESSURE

As I said earlier in discussing the putting grip, I don't believe in different pressure points in the hands. I don't buy the theory that says the club should be held more firmly with the last two or three fingers of the left and the middle fingers of the right. I think all eight fingers, the left thumb, and the two palms should be exerting the same amount of pressure. My only exception is that I don't feel the right thumb should be exerting any pressure. In the pitch shot or the full swing, the right thumb just sits on the club, taking a ride and exerting no influence. If you didn't need it to write with and to hold your fork, you could cut it off. The lack of pressure from the thumb helps avoid having the right hand (which is the stronger hand, if you are a right-hander, of course) take over, closing the clubface and ruining the shot.

The most important and most overlooked pressure point is that of the right palm against the left thumb. Maintaining constant pressure here is what keeps your hands joined during the swing, working together rather than in opposition.

As with the putt and the chip, the grip pressure should not be so tight as to cause tension in the arms and make you lose club-head speed, nor should it be loose so you lose control of the club.

Your grip pressure *will* tend to tighten during the swing, especially on a full shot, but your thought must be to keep the pressure constant from start to finish. This is especially critical in pitching or sand play, where a smooth swing is mandatory. Fortunately, it is easier to do, because the swing is shorter and easier and there is not the subconscious need for power that you might have with the driver. So when you practice the short game, in particular, concentrate on keeping your grip pressure the same throughout. Once the hands start tightening and grabbing, you're done.

THE SETUP

As you move into the ball from behind and to the side, you should set your weight evenly balanced between the two feet. At the same time the weight should be equally distributed between the balls of your feet and the heels. Do not let the weight get toward your toes, because from that position you can lose your balance and "come over the top." If your weight gets too far back on your heels, it restricts your ability to move your legs in an athletic manner. However, for the short shot it is better to have your weight more toward the heels than the toes. Your balance will be better, which is the primary consideration in the shot.

Your upper body should bend from the hips and your knees should flex slightly, somewhat as if you were sitting down on a stool. How much bend and how much flex will depend on the club you have in your hands. In all cases your arms should hang naturally without reaching for the ball, so you will be more erect with just a slight knee flex with a driver. With the sand wedge, the shortest club in your bag, you will be bent over more and your knees will be more flexed. As you bend more, the knees must flex more to stay balanced, your rear end acting as the counterbalance.

On the full swing your feet and body should be aligned square to the target line. For the pitch shot, however, you should set slightly open, your left foot pulled back from the line, to allow your hips to clear more easily in the shorter swing. The degree of openness will vary with the type of shot you are trying to play. Your feet will be closer together than for the full swing, just a few inches apart for the short pitch and gradually widening as the swing gets longer. As you need more distance, you need more platform for the swing, so your platform should widen.

Set Your Body with the Hill. For a steep downhill shot, align all parts of your body as much as possible with the slope, as shown.

For a normal pitch shot, the ball should be positioned in the center of the stance to slightly forward of center. You don't want to have it so far back that you are hitting down on it, nor should it be so far forward that you have to pick it. The ball should be basically at the bottom of your swing, your pendulum, where you can sweep it up in the air without working at it or beating on it. The position will vary for special shots, of course. If you are facing a slope and the ball is above your feet, it must be positioned farther away from you. Below your feet, it must be closer. From a tight lie or a downhill lie, play the ball back a little. From an uphill lie, play it forward. Experiment in practice until you get a feel for the correct positions under different circumstances. All these various ball positions apply to special shots that we'll examine later.

THE SWING

Leg action is just as important in the short shots as it is in the full swings. Leg action comes primarily from a rocking of the knees:

The Short Pitch Is a Short Swing. The swing for the short pitch shot is just a miniature of the full swing. Stand with your feet open to the target and swing the club back normally for the length of the shot. Be smooth and firm, not hard and fast, with the swing. Notice the slight action of the legs going back and coming into impact. It's important to think of making the follow-through as long as the backswing.

They rock to the right on the backswing as the weight goes to the right heel, then rock to the left on the forward swing as the weight goes first to the left toe and then to the left heel. This rocking action is timed with the swinging of the arms as the arms, legs, and body all move together. The longer the swing, the more pronounced is the action of the legs.

In either the full shot or the short shot, the movement of the legs provides the foundation for the swinging of the arms. In the pitch shot, the legs give you a momentum from the bottom up that lets you move the pendulum of your hands and arms smoothly.

It's important to remember what I said at the start of this chapter—the normal pitch shot is just a smaller version of your full swing. Don't try to change the arc or plane of your swing. Don't try to take it outside or inside, make it more upright, or make any other manipulations. Just swing normally, fitting the length of your swing to the distance required.

There are, of course, special shots that require special maneuvers. I'll cover them in this chapter and in the chapter on trouble shots.

PITCHING FUNDAMENTALS IN BRIEF

- The grip is the same as for the full swing. The Vardon grip is the most popular, but the interlocking and 10-finger grips also may be used. Unlike the putting and chipping grip, the two hands should work together.
- Your grip pressure should be uniform in both hands, except that there is no pressure from the right thumb; it should be light enough to avoid tension but firm enough to control the club, and it should remain constant throughout the swing.
- The setup is the same as for the full swing—weight balanced, bent slightly from the hips, knees slightly flexed, arms hanging naturally; your feet will be slightly open for the pitch shots.
- The swing is a miniature version of your full swing, rocking the knees in concert with the swinging of your arms.

The overall concept of pitching is just that—it's a pitch. While the chip shot is characterized by little loft and a lot of roll, the pitch shot is one with a lot of loft and very little roll. It is used when you need height to get the ball over a hazard, over irregular ground, over a fairway to a close-cut pin.

To successfully visualize and execute a pitch shot, I think of having the ball in my hand and tossing it up to the hole. I make an underhanded pitch. If I asked you to take a ball and pitch it 20 feet into a trash can, you wouldn't stand stiff-legged and straight and just make an arm movement. You would be very rhythmic. You would rock back and forward with your legs, at the same time swinging your arm back and through and up, and you would toss the ball high so it would fall into the can.

The Pitch Is an Underhand Toss. A good way to visualize the pitch-shot action is to imagine tossing a ball high in the air with an underhand motion. That's the same kind of motion you want to feel with a club in your hand.

That's how I visualize the pitch shot in golf, only now the release point is the clubhead instead of my hand. In my mind I see
the ball flying up, landing at a certain point on the green, and
rolling to the hole. I visualize a certain trajectory. If I don't have
much green to work with, I visualize the ball flying higher and
landing more softly, rolling more slowly to the hole. If I have
plenty of green between me and the cup, I visualize a lower trajectory with the ball rolling farther after it lands. Then I go ahead
and, with a particular image in mind, make that smooth, rhythmic swing.

Every player who is good around the greens has imagination.
He is able to see the shot he wants to play and then execute it. I
don't think you can be very successful without that kind of imagination, whether you have a putt, a chip, a pitch, or a sand shot.
The visualization gives you a feel for what you want to do. Then
you let your body reproduce that feel. It's amazing how many
times I visualize pitching a ball a certain height and see it land
on a specific spot, then have it happen exactly as I imagined it.

Visualization serves another purpose, especially when you face
a dangerous shot over water, sand, or other hazardous material.
It gives you a positive approach by taking your mind off the trouble that might await. If you are picturing the ball flying nicely

Visualizing the height
you want your pitch
shot to fly will help
you make the correct
swing.

onto the green and snuggling up to the hole, the trouble disappears. If there were a pit full of vipers between you and the green, what would you care? You're just going to pitch the ball stiff.

The Water Isn't There. Many golfers panic when a shot must carry over water. The best technique is to ignore the water and make a smooth, confident swing. Think about the underhand toss. Again, get the right hand more active and loft the ball over the hazard that, in your mind, isn't even there.

I have the mechanical ability to hit a pitch any way I want—high, low, hard, or soft. With practice you can develop that same ability. Then, as I approach a shot, I simply ask myself, "What is the easiest shot to get close from this particular position?" I make the determination, then I see the shot in my mind, and the visualization programs my body. Then I just let it happen. Once you have visualized the shot, you are 80 percent on the way toward executing it successfully.

Once I did it too successfully. In the 1970 PGA Championship at Southern Hills in Tulsa, I was in contention during the third round when I came to the par-5 sixteenth hole. There is a lake in front of the green, and I had to lay up short of it with my second shot. The pin was cut close to the front of the green. I visualized the shot I wanted to play and hit it perfectly. It looked like I had holed it. Instead, the ball hit the bottom of the flagstick and bounced back into the water. I made bogey on a shot with which I should have made eagle or birdie.

Still, I'd take my chances on that happening if I could hit such a good shot every time. Visualization is the difference between an artist and a mechanic. In the short game, especially in pitching, the artist will win every time. Once you become competent with the mechanics, develop your imagination so you, too, can become an artist.

Let's take a brief look at those mechanics.

I always use a sand wedge for pitching, and I recommend you do the same. You need as much loft as you can get when you are pitching anywhere from 10 to 60 yards out. I will grip down on the club for the shorter pitch shots, gradually going toward the end of the handle as I move back and make bigger swings.

Set the face of your sand wedge slightly open for the normal pitch shot, turning it 10 or 15 degrees to the right or clockwise. This position brings the bounce on the flange more into play and keeps the club from digging into the ground. It also adds a little loft to the club and the shot.

The execution is as I described earlier. Set up normally, your feet a little open to the line of your shot, and use a smaller version of your normal swing. Your arms hang naturally and the club becomes a pendulum, an extension of the arms and hands, as you swing it slowly and rhythmically, keeping your grip pressure reasonably light and constant throughout the swing. There is never any need to rush a pitch-shot swing. You don't need power for distance. You need smoothness for accuracy. Your weight must shift, so your knees must get involved—only slightly for the 10-yard pitch and gradually increasing as the shot gets longer.

For pitches of 10 and 20 yards or so, your feet are pretty close together. As you face the longer shots, say 40 yards and beyond, you need to widen your stance to provide that platform for the bigger swing. At 60 yards, which is about the maximum distance I can pitch the ball without resorting to a full, hard swing, I will be gripping at the end of the club, making a pretty full turn of the shoulders with plenty of knee action. But the swing is really no different than the short pitch. I'm still swinging it back and through—always remember to complete your follow-through—but longer. And because it is longer, of course, I will be generating more clubhead speed.

These are all the mechanics you need to know for the normal pitch shot. And if it sounds simple, it is. You don't need to do anything out of the ordinary. Just swing and clip the ball off the turf as you would any other shot.

Your only variables will be the firmness and speed of the green. You must learn to judge how far the ball is going to release and roll or how quickly it is going to stop on a particular surface. Guess how you learn that. Practice, of course.

The normal pitch shot flies at the height dictated by the loft of your club, has a normal amount of backspin, and will roll a reasonable amount on landing. It is played with the normal amount of "release"—in other words, your hands unhinge and rotate normally through impact, just as they do on the full swing. This shot is the basic weapon in your arsenal and will work for you on the majority of pitches you will face in the course of a round. But, once you become competent with it, there are two other types of shots that occasionally will come in handy and that you should learn. One is the low shot with extra spin. The other is the lob, an extra high shot that will settle on the green, as Sam Snead once said, "like a butterfly with sore feet." Interestingly enough, both are played essentially the same way.

The spin shot comes in handy under windy conditions, when you want to keep the ball low and unaffected by the breeze. It also

10 yards

30 yards

50 ya

Widen the Stance for Longer Pitches. As the pitch shot gets longer, the weight at address shifts from slightly to the left for the 10-yard shot to more balanced for the longer ones, and your feet should be placed progressively wider apart to provide a foundation for the increased length of swing.

is useful when you must stop the ball quickly and your lie is too tight to allow a lob shot. But there must be some length to the shot if you are going to spin the ball off a tight lie, because it requires clubhead velocity. I can hit a ball off cement and spin the daylights out of it from 30 yards, but I can't do it from 10 yards. If I get the clubhead moving fast enough to impart a lot of spin, the ball is going to carry too far. So be judicious in your use of this method.

The shot is played by positioning the ball slightly farther back in your stance, then increasing the speed of your right hand as you swing through, keeping the club going low and toward the target on the follow-through. The right hand does *not* turn over, thus closing the face. Feel as if you are slipping the face under the ball while keeping it square, not allowing it to close through impact. On this shot and the lob, you should feel as if the heel of the club is leading through impact—the toe never passes the heel. Keep the right hand cocked a little longer into the forward swing, then unload it quickly, really shooting it through impact.

Don't hit abruptly down on the ball. You want to nip the ball off the turf, just clipping the grass and not really taking a divot. It's

The normal pitch shot should not be made with a steeply descending swing that gouges out a deep divot *(top);* rather, the ball should be nipped off the turf *(bottom).*

To Loft a Shot, Use the Right and Stay Back. When you must loft a ball over a bunker or other hazard, remember the concept of a smooth swing. There is no need for distance. Accuracy and good contact are the goals. Visualize tossing the ball into the air with an underhand motion. Get more active with the right hand, using it to slide the clubface under the ball, and let your weight hang on the right side or at least centered as you swing into the follow-through.

as if you were hitting the ball with a knife, cutting the pants off it. The ball will balloon up the clubface, catching all the grooves. The fact that you have delofted the club a bit by playing the ball back will send the ball flying lower. The increased speed of the clubhead caused by the faster use of your right hand will impart a great deal more spin. So the ball will take one long bounce, then check up immediately.

Don't forget that the left hand has to keep going at the same time, but the force for the shot comes from the right.

The lob shot is useful when you must carry the ball over a bunker, water hazard, or rough and stop it quickly. You are stopping the ball with trajectory rather than spin.

This shot also is played with the right hand very active through impact, slipping the clubface under the ball as I just described. But now you want to play the ball more forward in your stance

and set your weight more on your right side at address. Drop the right shoulder a little, then stay on your right side as you swing through and *up*. Feel as if you are hanging back through impact, never letting the weight go to the left side. The speed of the right hand slipping the clubface under the ball will get the ball up and give it carry, and the arc of your swing, the fact that the club is going up through impact, will give the shot the height you need.

This shot is the only type on which I will lighten my grip, and only then if a particularly soft shot is called for. I think of it as a "loose-handed" grip, although I never lose control of the club. But lightening the grip will result in less of a hit and make the shot softer.

On this shot, as the right hand flashes the clubface under the ball, it actually passes the left hand. The left still leads, going down your intended line and giving you direction on the shot, but it actually breaks down or becomes concave as the right passes it through impact (but remember that the clubface doesn't close— the toe never passes the heel). The effect is a scooping action that sends the ball high with very little spin and lets it land softly on the green.

Again, look at the lie. The ball must have some grass under it
if you are going to play the lob shot successfully. It is impossible
to play the shot off hardpan, almost impossible to play it from a
tight lie, and very difficult to play it from even a normal lie. It is
a shot that must be played when the ball is sitting up nicely. It is
especially effective from higher grass where you have room to get
the clubhead under the ball.

The high lob shot is dangerous when
played off hardpan or from a tight lie; it
normally should be attempted only with a
good lie where there is plenty of grass
under the ball or from a fluffy lie with
the ball sitting reasonably well.

NO (HARDPAN)

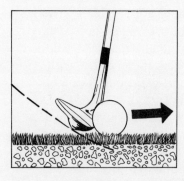

NO (TIGHT LIE)

YES BUT DIFFICULT (NORMAL)

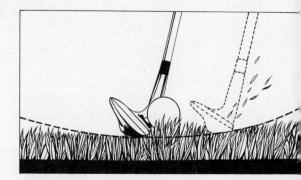

YES (FLUFFY)

Swing Abruptly Up and Down for Quick Loft. If you face a shot from a greenside hollow or some other situation that requires you to get the ball up quickly, pick the club up more abruptly on the backswing and swing it down into the ball on a steeper angle. Again slide the clubface quickly under the ball with your right hand, making your follow-through as steep as your downswing. This will pop the ball high into the air.

For every shot, your first consideration should be the lie. It almost always determines the shot you can play—at least the one you can play wisely with the best chance of success.

Both the lob shot and the spin shot I have just described require practice before you use them in actual play. But you knew I was going to say that, didn't you?

Another warning here—once you learn these shots, don't abuse the use of them. Don't play them where they aren't needed. I see that so often. I teach a player the lob shot and he becomes infatuated with it. Instead of playing a normal 30-yard pitch that will satisfy the requirements perfectly, he wants to lob the ball, a much more difficult shot. It can cost a lot more strokes than the appropriate use of the shot will save.

Always play the easiest shot for the task at hand, the simplest shot the situation allows. Why make things difficult? I and most of my peers know all the shots. At least we think we do. But we play the one that is called for. We choose the easiest shot that will get the ball close.

As a corollary, if the situation calls for a shot that you don't have, that you haven't practiced yet, then go to the next best shot that *is* in your repertoire. This goes back to the business of not exceeding your limitations. Playing the shot you can handle, even if it won't get you quite as close, is better than duffing a shot that you can't make.

These decisions require judgment that comes from experience and practice, of course, but it starts with that one premise—take the easy road.

Pitch shots, of course, often are played out of rough, and you must be aware of what high grass can do to a club and subsequently to the shot. Grasses vary in their coarseness and consistency. Bermuda grass, found mostly in the south, is the toughest of the most common grasses. Rye grass, often used to overseed southern courses in the winter, also is a strong, sticky grass. When you land in these grasses, or any rough, and face a pitch to the green, the first thing to look for is the direction of the grain. If the grain is running against you, if the grass is lying opposite the direction of your shot, you must make a bigger swing, accelerating the club through the grass and making sure you maintain its momentum. Just hit the ball harder. If you don't, the grass will simply grab the club and take it away from you, and you will end up leaving the ball short of the green, in the bunker or still in the rough.

In this case, the longer your shot and the bigger your swing, the better off you are. If you have a delicate little shot that only has to travel 15 or 20 feet to the green, you have a major problem.

The best method for escape may be the explosion shot, which

we'll discuss further in the chapters on sand play and trouble shots. But your first step is to be aware of how rough, especially if it is growing against you, can stifle your shot.

Finally, it's important to select the right sand wedge for your pitch shots. Ideally, you would choose one that also is good for play out of sand. For the skilled player, this choice is not too difficult. In both cases, you need a wedge that has a flange (the bottom part of the club) that is not too wide and that does not have excessive "bounce." Bounce is determined by the amount that the trailing edge of the flange drops below the leading edge. It helps

If rough is growing in the direction of the shot, the ball will come out easier and faster; if it is against that direction, the grass will resist the club, so you must swing harder.

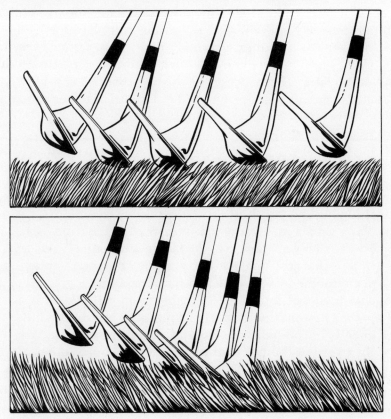

the club skid through the turf on a pitch shot and through the sand in a bunker. But, while a club with a lot of bounce may be good for sand play, depending on the consistency of the sand, it won't be good for pitching.

The professional, skilled in both pitching and sand play, may prefer a medium-width flange with minimal bounce in all cases. But this club may not be suitable for the higher-handicap player. The wider flange may give him a better all-around club. Remember, the wider the flange, the less bounce you need. The narrower the flange, the more bounce there should be on the club.

Most sand wedges are reasonably well suited to both pitching and sand play, although very few are excellent for both. My advice is to find a knowledgeable professional who is familiar with your game and have him recommend a club that best fits your needs. But do it. The right equipment can save you a lot of strokes.

In recent years we have seen the advent of more-lofted wedges, 60 or 62 degrees compared to the normal 56- or 57-degree club. If you face a lot of high, soft pitches on your course, or have a lot of deep bunkers, or if your greens are hard and fast, consider getting one. The club will produce shots with a higher trajectory that land softer and, if you learn to use it properly, can save you strokes. I normally don't carry one, but I'm forced to put one in my

---

THE PITCH SHOT IN BRIEF

- The pitch is like an underhand toss of the ball; imagine throwing the ball high in the air into a trash can.
- The good player around the green has imagination; visualize the shot you want to play; then let the body react to that image, that will give you the positive approach to playing over trouble; it will make you an artist, not a mechanic.
- The low shot with spin and the high, soft lob both are played by making the right hand more active; the difference is in the ball position and shape of the swing arc.
- Be aware of the effect of high grass on your pitches.
- Choose a well-designed wedge that can be used both for pitching and for sand play.

bag occasionally, especially when we play some of the new sta-
dium-type courses with their deep bunkers and steep embank-
ments. If you didn't have a highly lofted wedge on those courses,
you would have to play some shots backward. Sometimes I think
we may have to increase the 14-club limit just to be able to play
the ridiculous shots some of these new courses demand.

You now have the tools to learn and become competent in executing the three basic pitch shots. With these shots in your bag, and
with your awareness of visualization and its benefits, you are well
equipped to handle sand play and trouble shots, the two areas that
will round out your short-game expertise.

5

RELAX, HERE'S HOW
TO MASTER THE SAND

Ranking right up there with the fear of flying, the fear of heights, and other phobias is, at least among golfers, the fear of sand. On courses around the world every weekend you can hear the frightened cry, "Stay out of the bunker, please!!" The sand is the last place most amateur golfers want to be.

Yet on the PGA Tour, when a shot strays from the flag and starts heading toward rough stuff, the player always mutters, "Get in the bunker!" You see, the good player knows that a shot from sand usually is easier and can be executed more consistently than a shot from the high grass that surrounds most greens.

Late on Saturday in the third round of the 1986 U.S. Open at Shinnecock, I was very frustrated. I had been playing beautifully from tee to green and wasn't getting much out of the round. I had done the same thing the day before. Even though I had shot 68, I had played much better than I had scored, and I was upset. Now I was doing the same thing.

On the fifteenth, a par-4 of about 400 yards, I drove into the rough and drew a terrible lie. Because of the lie, the wind, and my position on the hole, I didn't think I could get the ball on the green from there, so I tried to put it in the front bunker. I thought that would be the best place from which to play my third shot.

When I walked into the bunker, the look of the shot was perfect, slightly uphill, just what I needed. I said to myself, "Damn, let's hole it out of here." As soon as I hit it, I knew it was in. When I shook my fist as I came out of the bunker, it was not so much in triumph as it was to signal the end of the frustration I'd been feeling for two days.

The shot turned the day around. I finished with 70 and went on to win the next day by two strokes. Converting a possible bogey into a birdie on that fifteenth hole was, it turned out, my margin of victory.

I'm not necessarily advocating that you *try* to hit your ball into the bunker, although it truly is a better place from which to play than heavy rough if you have the ability and confidence to do it.

Confidence is paramount. I don't want to sound boastful, but I believe I can get into a bunker with any man alive and not come out second. I think any good bunker player has to feel that way to produce good shots under all conditions.

I think the greatest bunker shot I ever played was on the par-5 ninth hole at the Players Club during the first or second year we had the Tournament Players Championship there. I had tried to hit my third shot with a wedge in tight to a pin that was only about 10 feet from the edge of the green. I missed and the ball bounced down a bank into the back of a deep bunker with a steep front wall. Now I had about 15 feet to carry over a 6-foot wall with the pin just beyond on a very hard green.

I was playing with Bruce Lietzke at the time, and I heard him say, "I know the guy is good, but I want to see him play this one." And he walked over to the edge of the bunker to watch.

I was carrying a 60-degree wedge with very little flange because the bunkers there were hard. I flipped the wedge under the ball, zipped it over the wall, and as soon as it left the sand I knew I had holed it. The ball hit a foot onto the green, took the backspin, and leaped into the cup.

Lietzke was mesmerized.

I only tell that story to make a point. I was not afraid of the shot. Of course I didn't expect to hole it, but I was confident that I could get it close. I knew I had the ability, because I had worked countless hours and days and years to develop it.

I've been named Sand Player of the Year on three occasions by *Golf* magazine, an honor determined by vote of the Tour players, so I guess I know something about getting out of bunkers. Maybe it's because I get in so many of them. But anybody who plays much golf is going to get in a lot of them, too, so he had better find a way to consistently play the ball out and onto the green, hopefully with a chance for a one-putt. I can help you develop the ability and confidence to do that. You might not become a Tour-caliber bunker player, unless you are willing to put in the practice time that the rest of us have. But I'll guarantee that if you digest what I say in this chapter, you'll be able to get out of the bunker in an acceptable manner without having a heart attack.

You need a method to get the ball from sand repetitively and well, and it must be one that incorporates some kind of blast or explosion shot. Picking and putting out of sand usually doesn't work unless the bunker is flat with no lip, and you don't see many of those around.

Let me quickly mention a few different techniques. One technique I call the skimming method, which calls for more of a wide, shallow swing, taking a very shallow cut of sand very close to the back of the ball. Ken Venturi, among other good players, is an advocate of this style. He almost (but not quite) picks the ball off the sand. Kenny has described it as "clipping the ball off a carpet." It's an excellent method from good lies and when the sand is shallow and firm. Properly executed, the shot puts a lot of spin on the ball. But I feel it's rather dangerous for most players, mainly because you must strike the sand so close to the ball.

The opposite method is one in which a steep, V-shaped swing is used, striking down farther behind the ball and making a steep entry into the sand. The club cuts deeply under the ball and throws out a lot of sand. Gary Player, Lee Trevino, and Billy Casper, among others, use this method, which is very good from poor lies and deep, softer sand. Because it lets you strike farther behind the ball, it allows a great margin for error, but because of the steep angle you have to be careful not to leave the club in the sand. I think you have to work too hard with this method, because you are digging out a lot of sand, and I don't use it myself. But the three guys I just mentioned are among the best sand players in history, so who am I to say it's wrong?

I use what I call the explosion method, as do many good players, and I recommend it for you. It is more or less a compromise between the two styles I've just described. I think it's the easiest method with the least chance for error.

You will encounter many different kinds of shots in a bunker. The explosion method, with variations, will handle all of them. I can play any kind of bunker shot I desire. I can play a low, running shot, a low shot that spins, a high lob, a high shot that spins. I can hit 10 inches behind a ball in a footprint and pop it out nicely. I literally can take a 4-wood into the sand and play a pretty decent shot onto the green.

I will instruct you in the basics, for the normal sand shot and most of the variations you will encounter. But I can't emphasize enough that you're going to have to wade into that practice bunker and work hard to become proficient in the various techniques.

THE NORMAL SAND SHOT

First, let's get rid of your fear. Most amateur players are afraid of the sand for two related reasons: The shot is an unknown, one they don't know how to handle because they don't know the proper technique to use; and they seldom, if ever, practice it, probably because they don't know how to do it in the first place. Let me explain how to do it, which will take care of both problems.

The normal sand shot, one in which the ball is sitting reasonably well on top of the sand and on a reasonably level surface, is really a pretty easy shot. I know you've heard that before, and you probably don't believe it, but it's true. It's one that does not require precise club-to-ball contact and so allows a considerable margin for error. (The fluff shot from high grass and the shot from water are the other two, but sand is much more consistent than grass, and the water shot . . . well, it should be tried only under the most desperate circumstances.)

All sand shots require that you create an explosion of sand that carries the ball out. Think of having a handful of sand with the ball perched on top, then just making an underhand toss out of the bunker. That same motion removes the ball from the sand with a club, only now the clubface sliding through the sand creates the handful of sand with the ball sitting on top.

With the explosion method, all you are trying to do is to get the

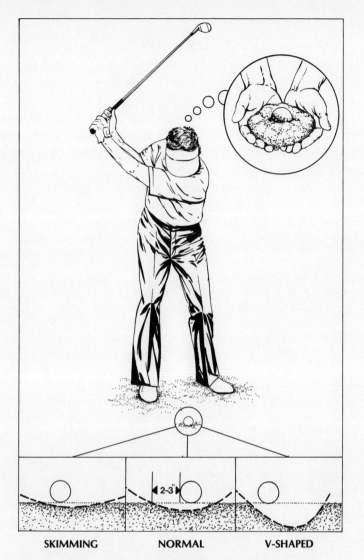

SKIMMING   **NORMAL**   **V-SHAPED**

The three basic techniques for playing from sand are, from left, the method of skimming or making a shallow cut and entering the sand close to the ball, the normal method in which the club enters two to three inches behind the ball and makes a slightly deeper cut, and the blast method in which the ball is gouged out by making a deeper, more V-shaped cut.

clubface under the ball. Anytime you can do that, you can get the ball in the air and out of the bunker. No matter how deeply the ball is buried, if you can get the club under it, it will get up.

You want your clubhead to enter the sand 2 to 3 inches behind the ball. This distance can vary with the consistency of the sand and some other factors that I will address, but it's a good guideline. I hear players talking about hitting an inch behind the ball, but I think that's too close. It doesn't give you enough margin for error. If you get a little closer or your club skids, you could blade the ball right over the green.

The spot where you want the club to first contact the sand will be your focal point as you address the ball. And, with a reasonably good swing, your club can contact the sand an inch or so in either direction and you still will achieve satisfactory results. That

The Sand Shot Is a Pitch Shot. The normal sand shot, as shown here, requires basically the same swing as a pitch shot. In this case, set your feet slightly open to the target, the left foot pulled back, your weight set slightly to the left. Open the clubface 30 to 35 degrees or so, until it is pointing at the target. Focus on a point two or three inches behind the ball, then swing the club back along your stance line and down and through the sand. As the flange of the club rides through the sand, the ball will be exploded out. Your follow-through is critical. Concentrate on making it as long as your backswing.

won't happen with a normal pitch or chip, and that's the luxury you have with a shot from sand.

The swing and setup are basically the same as I described for the high pitch shot. You don't have to cock the club up quickly as you do with the digging type shot, nor do you have to concentrate on a wider, shallower arc. Swing the club normally except for special situations that I will describe later, and even then you don't have to make drastic adjustments.

Generally you hold your sand wedge at the end of the handle with a normal grip and normal grip pressure, neither too tight nor too loose. Set up with a slightly open stance, your left foot pulled back or a little to the left of your target line. Wiggle your feet into the sand, distributing your weight as you would for a pitch shot, slightly to the left. By working your feet into the sand you establish a solid foundation and prevent slipping, which can be disastrous during the swing. This way is also good for testing the texture of the sand, determining how soft or firm it is. You

can't test any other way because you are not allowed to ground your club in the sand before the shot.

Open the clubface about 30 or 35 degrees to allow the flange or bounce—remember, that's the bottom portion of the club that on a sand wedge hangs below the leading edge—to work properly.

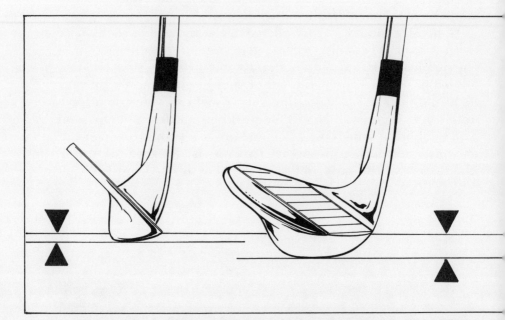

The "bounce" on the flange of the club rides through the sand under the ball and keeps the leading edge from digging in.

The clubface should be open to your *stance line,* which is point-ing to the left of your target, but the face should be pointing at your target, which is the flag or wherever you want the ball to start. Then swing the club back along your stance line, a little to the outside of your target line and on an upright plane. It will come back down across and to the inside of your target line on the follow-through, but because the clubface is aimed at the target, the ball will start there. It's not something you have to worry about. During the swing, keep your eyes focused on that point 2 or 3 inches behind the ball. Be a little wristy, letting the hands hinge and unhinge freely, and use your right hand to send the clubhead down and underneath the ball and up again in a slicing action. The impact will force the sand up, carrying the ball with it.

To play the bunker shot, the feet should be set open or to the left of the target line; the clubface should be aimed at the target and the swing should be along the stance line.

The action of the right hand is similar to that when you are trying to spin a pitch shot, only in this case the club will come up after cutting through the sand, finishing high. Remember, you never want the toe to pass the heel—always feel as if the heel of the club is leading from start to finish. If the club turns over, it will stick in the sand.

The finish is critically important. Do not let the club stop in the sand, because if you do the ball will stop there too. A good rule of thumb is to make your follow-through as long as your backswing.

The consistency of the sand—how coarse or fine it is, how soft or firm—has a great effect on the shot. With practice, you will learn how to handle it. In coarser, more firmly packed sand, the ball will come out hotter and travel farther, so you swing easier; soft, fluffy sand tends to deaden the impact, so you must create more speed with a longer swing.

Practice also will help you determine how much swing speed— thus, how long a swing—you need to carry the ball certain distances from sand of certain consistencies.

The arc of your swing—how steep or shallow it is—also determines the height and length of your shot. The ball will come out of the sand at about the same angle that the club enters the sand. To get a higher, shorter shot, make a steeper, more sharply descending entry into the sand. For a lower, longer shot, make a shallower, more sweeping entry.

In general, shots from the sand should carry about three-quarters of the way to the hole and roll the rest of the way. Thus, on a 60-foot shot you should try to carry the ball 45 feet and let it roll 15 feet. That will vary, of course, depending on the slope from which you are playing and the lie of the ball, which I'll discuss later. On certain shots, when you have a good lie on firm sand, you also can make a shallower cut closer to the ball that will apply more spin and stop the ball more quickly.

I'm sorry to have to keep mentioning practice, but there is no secret to playing this game well. Knowing and using the proper technique can improve your sand play immediately, but to master all the subtleties and become a really proficient player, you must spend some time in that practice bunker. And, by the way, be sure to hit some practice bunker shots every time before you play a strange course.

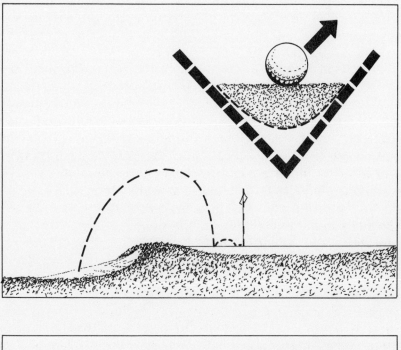

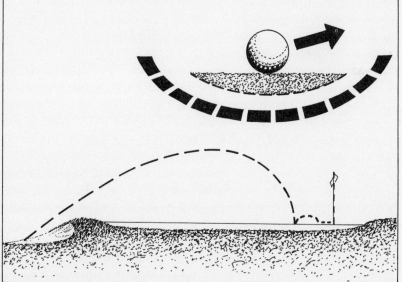

A steep, narrow swing arc *(top)* results in a higher, shorter shot; a wide, shallow arc produces a longer, lower shot.

The technique I've described will work well on most of the bunker shots you encounter. On those troublesome "other" shots that you occasionally will face, the explosion method is still the one, but with some variations.

Before I get to those, let me give you one basic guideline for all sand shots—always align your body with the slope, setting your shoulder parallel with the contour. If you have a level lie at the bottom of the bunker, set up normally. On a downhill lie, dig in with your lower leg, set the shoulders down accordingly, and swing down the slope. On an uphill lie, reverse the procedure, again digging in the lower leg, setting the shoulders up in line with the contour, and swinging up the slope.

This body alignment will help you swing with the contour, up or down, which is what you want to do.

Let's examine the different shots you might encounter.

THE BURIED LIE

The ball that is plugged or partially buried in the sand seems to be everybody's nightmare, but there is no reason for it to be if you understand the technique.

If the ball happens to be buried on the level, just swing down into it on a steeper angle, setting the weight a bit more left and making the swing a little more up and down. Do not close or hood the clubface. I play virtually every shot with an open face. The most I ever close it is to square, which you might want to do if the ball is quite buried and the shot is a long one.

If you have a "fried egg" with a wide crater, try to strike at the edge of the crater with greater force. If the ball is plugged cleanly, the shot is not as difficult. Just get the club underneath it on a more downward angle and it will come out nicely. But it will come out lower with little spin and will roll relatively longer, so allow for that if you can. You want to be sure of getting the ball out, but you often don't have to swing as hard at a buried ball as you might think.

Many buried lies occur on the front wall of a bunker, when we have gone for a close-cut flag and come up a bit short. In this case, adjust your body to the contour of the wall, set the clubface open, and simply swing into the sand 2 or 3 inches behind or at the edge

Strike the Crater. If the ball is buried or you have a "fried egg" lie, as shown here, swing more steeply and try to strike the sand at the back edge of the crater around the ball.

of the crater, popping the ball out. This shot too will come out hotter with little spin, but it will be higher and so will run commensurately less.

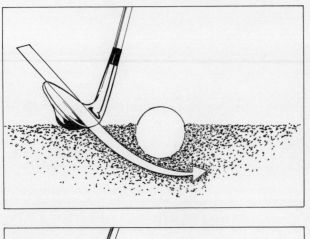

When the ball is plugged in the sand *(top),* the club should enter the sand close to the ball on a steep arc; for a "fried egg" lie, strike the sand at the back edge of the crater, again with a steep arc.

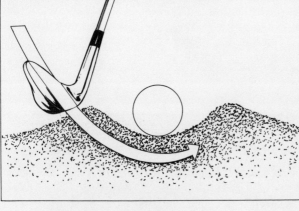

THE DOWNHILL LIE

If your ball catches on the back side of the bunker, on the downhill slope, play it as I indicated earlier. Set your shoulders parallel with the slope, the weight on your lower leg. Your swing will necessarily be steeper, and your objective is still to swing the clubface through under the ball.

In this situation, the ball will always come out lower and run

On the Downhill, Swing Down. From a downhill lie in the bunker, again align your body with the slope. Play the ball back in your stance, pick the club up more abruptly going back and swing down the slope. The ball will come out lower and roll farther when it hits the green, so allow for this if possible.

farther once it hits the green. Also, a ball caught on a slope usually is partially buried, compounding the problem. You won't be able to put much, if any, spin on it, so it will run even farther than normal. If you have a long way to go, this might not be a problem. If the pin is cut close, don't try to finesse a shot and get the ball close. Getting it out and on the green is your first consideration.

THE UPHILL LIE

This presents the opposite problem from the downhill lie, but it usually is easier to handle. Again align your shoulders with the slope, your weight on your lower leg, and swing with the slope. In this case you would be swinging *up,* taking a normal cut of sand. Because you have effectively increased the loft on your sand wedge, the shot will fly higher and shorter, making it easier to control than the downhill shot, but you must remember to hit it harder to get it to the hole.

THE MEDIUM-LENGTH SHOT

For a 40–50-foot sand shot, the technique is the same but the stance simply gets wider, the swing gets longer, and the plane of the swing gets shallower; it's not as much of an up-and-down motion, because the sand needs to carry the ball out lower and farther rather than up and down.

THE LONG EXPLOSION

The same technique is employed for a shot of up to 20 or 30 yards, but the arc widens and flattens even more. There is less use of the right hand. Still strike 2 or 3 inches behind the ball, but the longer, harder swing and the shallower path of the club through the sand will carry the ball farther. The longer the shot, of course, the closer to the ball you will have to enter the sand. For the very long sand shot you might almost have to nip the ball off the surface, and that's where it gets chancy. I can comfortably play an explo-

Set and Swing with the Slope. When you face an uphill lie, set your shoulders and body in line with the slope as much as possible, then just swing with the slope, striking the sand behind the ball and following through to explode it out.

Remember that the shot will come out higher and shorter, so you must hit it harder to get it to the hole.

For the Long Explosion, the Swing Is Shallower. From a normal lie in the sand, the basic technique applies no matter how long the shot. But for the longer explosion shot, as shown in these sequences, the arc of the swing must widen and flatten, which makes the swing shallower. Set your weight balanced, not leaning to the left. Don't be as active with your right hand. Still strike the sand two or three inches behind the ball, but the longer, harder swing and the shallower path of the clubhead through the sand will carry the ball farther.

sion shot up to 45 yards. You'll have to determine for yourself how far you can hit the ball with that method. Then you will have to try something different, which I'll discuss in the next chapter.

THE SHORT EXPLOSION

For the shorter shot you should also contact the sand a little closer to the ball. Your swing won't be as long or hard, so you can't displace as much sand. If the consistency of the sand and the lie allow it, striking closer and cutting out a shallower layer of sand will help you spin the ball and stop it quicker.

THE WET BUNKER SHOT

This is not as difficult as it appears; because the sand is wet and more compacted, the ball will come out more quickly with more spin. Use your normal technique but try to cut the sand out a little closer to the ball and don't swing as long or as hard.

THE HIGH SPINNER

If you face a situation where, for example, you are in the front of a large bunker and must carry the ball over to a pin that is 12 feet over the lip, this shot is the only one that will work. You not only need to hit the ball high but must spin it as well. So open up the club more than usual and, with a wristy swing, try to hit the sand as close as possible to the ball and flick it out, sending the right hand under and through as we've discussed earlier. It's a risky shot, so practice it first, of course.

* * *

Playing from the bunker is no different than playing any other shot. You still must visualize, seeing in your mind how the shot will fly and where it will end up, then letting your body react to that image. I holed the shot in the Open at Shinnecock because I visualized it and had no doubt about my ability to execute the stroke correctly.

On the other hand, if you step up to a sand shot and are concerned only with somehow digging the ball out, you don't have a chance to get it close and, more often than not, probably will either leave it in the bunker or skull it over the green into further trouble. But if you are confident you can get the ball out with a smooth, easy swing, then let the visualization process take over. Good things will happen.

As critical as the technique you use, or maybe even more important, is the selection of your sand wedge. You must match the construction of your wedge, the width and "bounce" of its flange, with the kind of sand from which you are playing. The wedge with a thin flange and not much bounce is ideal for firm, compacted sand. The wedge with a wide flange and a lot of bounce is best for fine, powdery sand. Keep in mind that the wider the flange, the less bounce you need, and vice versa. If you have a club with a narrow flange and very little bounce, you have a pitching wedge, and it will tend to dig into the sand. The wedge with a medium-width flange and medium bounce obviously is best for all-around play, and it's the one you might normally want to use. It also is probably the best kind of club for pitching the ball from grass. But it wouldn't hurt to have the others on hand for special conditions.

The 60-degree wedge, which usually comes with a wide flange and not much bounce, is good out of soft sand. My sand wedge is 58 degrees, which is a compromise of sorts, and you might want to try something like that.

As with the wedge for pitching, it's best to experiment and find which works best for you.

Now, armed with the proper equipment and the knowledge of technique, you are ready to lose your fear of the sand and develop the ability to get the ball out and close on a regular basis. All you need to do is . . . well, you know by now what you need to do.

SAND PLAY IN BRIEF

- Conquer your fear of sand; bunker shots are really among the easiest in golf.
- Use the explosion method, slicing sand from under the ball and sending the ball out with it. Anytime you can get the club under the ball you can get the ball in the air and out of the bunker.
- Contact the sand 2 or 3 inches behind the ball, depending on the shot; an inch behind is too close.
- Set up with your stance open, pointing to the left, and your clubface pointing to the target.
- Swing back and through along your stance line, using your normal pitching swing except in unusual circumstances. If anything, make the swing a little wristier, the right hand sending the clubface under the ball, but always keep the heel of the club leading.
- Swing down and underneath the ball and up; your follow-through should be approximately as long as your back-swing.
- The consistency of the sand will affect how far the ball travels—farther from coarser, firmer sand and shorter from soft, fluffy sand, so adjust your swing length and speed accordingly.
- The ball will exit the sand at approximately the same angle at which the clubhead enters.
- For all shots, normal and unusual, set your shoulders and your body parallel to the slope of the bunker; then swing along that slope.
- Visualize the shot you want to hit and trust your body to react.
- Choose a sand wedge with the correct flange width and bounce for the sand on your course.

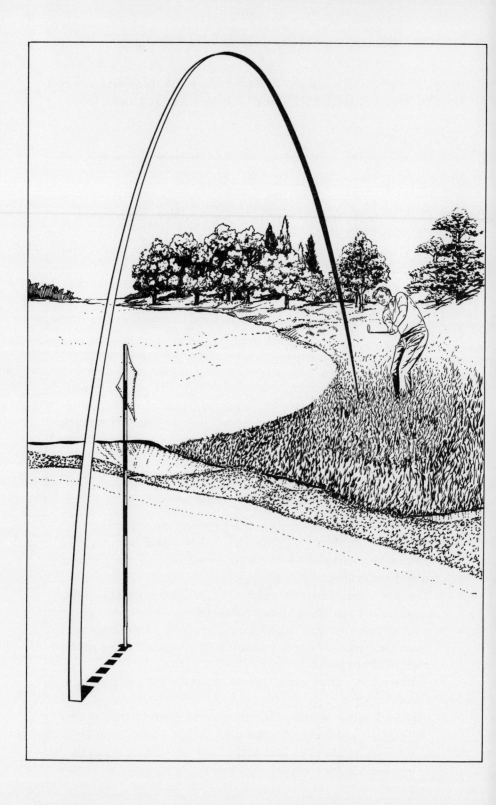

6

SPECIAL SHOTS
How to Play from Weird Places

Because it is not played on a uniform surface, golf is the most unpredictable of games. Sooner or later, usually more often than we like, we all wind up in spots that require something other than our normal swings to make the necessary shot. These special shots become especially critical the closer we get to the green, and the solutions to them become even more valuable in saving strokes. These shots also give us a chance to be creative, especially with our short shots, and that's what makes golf so much fun.

Following is a potpourri of unusual recovery shots and some advice on how to deal with them. You probably have faced them all or certainly will if you continue to play long enough. All the trouble shots aren't here. To cover every eventuality would take more pages than we have in this book. Besides, I don't know them all. There are enough ways to get in trouble in golf to fill a catalog. It seems like I see a new way every time out.

That's why imagination, coupled with practice, is so valuable. Know what shots you can make with the various clubs. Be aware of trajectories and shapes, how you can maneuver the ball with them (and how you can't, of course). Then be creative in getting out of some spot you have never been in before. Study your op-

tions, visualize the shot that will let you recover, then let your swing handle it.

The cardinal rule, of course, is to take the easiest way out, always. Don't make things harder on yourself than you have to. I've said that before in this book, but it bears repeating. Choose the shot that is most effective and is, at the same time, the one you have the best chance of executing at the moment with the least possible penalty if it should fail.

THE SHOT FROM HIGH ROUGH AROUND THE GREEN

Whether you are in a small grass pot bunker or just stuck in rough somewhere around a green, if the ball is buried in the grass you usually must play a type of explosion shot to get it out, up, and on the green. The blades of grass are entrapping the ball. If you try to strike the ball first, the grass will catch the clubhead and muffle

Explode from High Grass. The shot from a grass bunker or any high rough should be played the same as a sand shot—it should be exploded. Set your stance open to the target, open the clubface 30 to 35 degrees, and take the club back by swinging your arms along your stance line. The length of your backswing is determined by the length of the shot. Strike the grass a couple of inches behind the ball, letting the right hand send the clubface under the ball but making sure the face doesn't close. As with the sand shot, it is important that you follow through and don't let the clubhead stop in the grass.

the shot. You'll end up facing the same shot over again. So play it like a sand shot, the clubface never touching the ball. The principle is the same, only in this case the grass, not the sand, will lift the ball out.

First align your body with the contour of the ground, just as you do in the sand. Then aim at a point a couple of inches behind the ball and make the same swing as you would in the sand. Make the right hand active to get the clubhead underneath the ball and achieve the altitude you need for a successful shot.

If you want the ball to come out high and softly, open the clubface and swing through just as in the sand. If your situation dictates a lower shot that runs more, or if you need distance more than height, play it with a square clubface and drive the clubhead

On a pitch from high rough, attempting to strike the ball first *(top)* will send the ball out on too low a trajectory and may leave it in the grass; instead, play an explosion shot *(bottom)*, opening the clubface and sliding it through the grass under the ball as in a sand shot.

through the ball, still aiming a couple of inches behind it.

One of the greatest pitches I ever hit came in just such a situation. I came to the par-4 seventeenth hole in the final round of the 1981 Doral-Eastern Open with a one-shot lead over David Graham. I hit my drive into a fairway bunker and my second shot into heavy rough to the right and short of a bunker. The ball was submerged in tough, deep Bermuda grass, the worst kind of grass to play from. I had to go over the bunker to a hard green and a pin cut close to the near edge.

My first thought was that I did not want to leave the ball in the bunker and risk making double-bogey and losing the tournament. A bogey would still leave me tied for the lead, so I had to make sure I got the ball on the green. That, by the way, is a good thought in any trouble situation—*don't risk losing two strokes by trying to save one.*

I took my wedge, laid it open, and played the high, soft shot I just described. The ball came out perfectly, finished 8 feet past the hole, and I made the putt for a par. Then I went on to hit the tee shot on the eighteenth hole that I described in chapter 1 and I won the tournament.

I won the tournament with that shot on the seventeenth. But, more important, I didn't lose it there.

THE SHOT FROM A POT BUNKER WITH COMPACTED SAND

Pot bunkers used to be found mostly in Scotland and Ireland and on a few other links-type courses around the world. Lately, they, or the equivalent, are cropping up on more and more of the new courses in the United States.

Whether you are in a real pot bunker or facing a steep wall and the sand is firm or compacted, the problem is the same. You must get the ball up quickly from a tight lie.

To do it, use all the loft you have. Play either a 60-degree wedge or open your regular sand wedge totally. Use a wristy move with a lot of right hand and explode behind the ball, about an inch rather than the usual 2 inches because the sand is so firm, to get the ball up quickly over the face of the bunker. Slip the clubface under the ball and the hard sand will kick the ball upward.

PUTT WITH YOUR WEDGE

When your ball is nestled against the collar of grass surrounding
the green, it's difficult to hit it squarely with a putter blade or to
chip it, because the club usually catches and hangs up in the

Putt with Your Wedge from the Collar. When your ball is nestled
against the collar of grass surrounding the green, or when it is sitting
a few inches back into that collar, it's difficult to hit it squarely with a
putter blade or to chip it, because the club usually catches and hangs
up in the higher grass. The answer is to "putt" the ball with the
leading edge of your sand wedge, using your regular putting grip and
stance, soling the club lightly on top of the grass, making your normal
putting stroke, and catching the ball right in the belly—at or just
above the equator—so it will come out low and rolling. (See overleaf.)

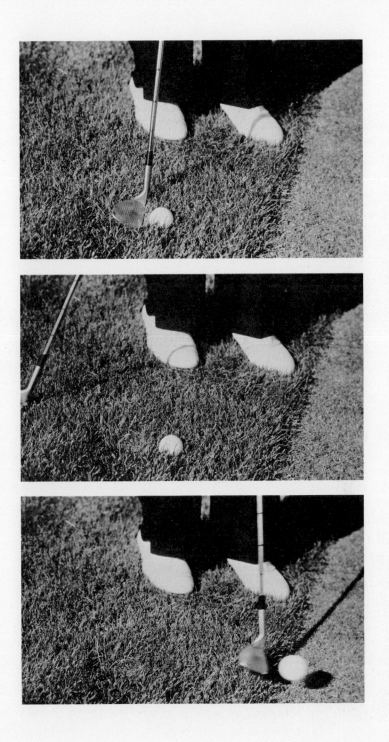

higher grass. The answer is to "putt" the ball with the leading edge of your sand wedge, using your regular putting grip and stance, soling the club lightly on top of the grass, making your normal putting stroke and catching the ball right in the belly, as close to the equator as you can. The same stroke can be used when the ball is sitting a few inches back into the collar. The force of the blow will pop the ball through the higher grass and get it rolling on the green. As with any putt or chip, keep your head still and your eyes focused on the back of the ball.

THE DOWNHILL FLUFF SHOT

Your ball goes through the green into a bank of rough beyond. You're now on a severely slanted lie facing a shot to very little putting surface. To solve the problem, align your body with the slope. Play the ball back in your stance, open the face of your sand wedge, pick the club up, and swing down the bank; play a wristy explosion shot, swinging the club into the grass behind the ball, popping it onto the fringe and letting it trickle down to the hole.

THE PICK SHOT FROM SAND

In my opinion, the hardest shot in golf is the 50- or 60-yard shot from a bunker. You are too far to explode and too close to hit a full shot. To play the shot, grip down on your sand wedge, hold it lightly, position the ball in the center of your stance, and pick the ball off the sand. Be sure the lie is good and be sure to hit the ball first.

THE SHOT FROM HARDPAN

Pitching the ball from hard, compacted dirt, such as at the start of a car-path or other packed-down area, can be tricky business. Trying to hit a normal pitch risks blading the ball or chunking it. I don't know anybody good enough to make that shot very often. I know I'm not. And because you're around the green, there almost always will be a bunker of some sort between you and the green,

From Downhill Rough, Play a Fluff. From a severely slanting lie with the ball in high grass close to the green, hit a "fluff" shot. Set your body with the slope, open the face of your sand wedge, and play a wristy explosion shot, swinging the club into the grass behind the ball, popping it up and letting it trick onto the green. Be sure to pick the club up more abruptly than normal and swing down the slope.

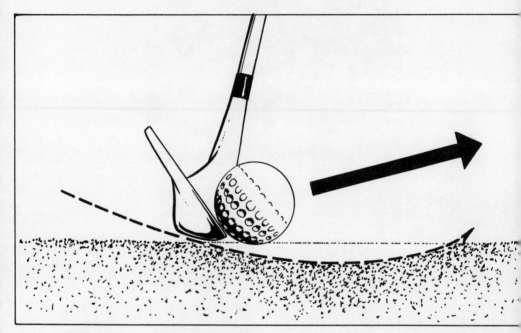

When playing the pick shot from sand, be sure to contact the ball first.

so that eliminates picking or chipping the ball. The answer is an "explosion" shot with a sand wedge, hitting close behind the ball with a firm and wristy swing. Use the right hand to make the clubhead skid under the ball, kicking up dirt that throws the ball into the air.

You can't hit 2 or 3 inches behind the ball as if it were on loose sand. You must strike the dirt within an inch or less of the ball ... but you *must* get some dirt, get the clubhead under the ball, and literally explode it out. You don't have to make a hard swing. The ball will travel almost as far as if it were a normal pitch. But the swing must be firm and aggressive.

So don't be afraid of the shot. Let your wrists unload and strike firmly just behind the ball, creating the explosion that gets it in the air.

From Hardpan, Play It as Sand. From hard, compacted dirt, the shot must be played as a sand shot, with some minor variations. Strike only an inch or so behind the ball instead of two or three inches. The swing doesn't have to be hard, because the ball will fly up "hot" from such a lie, but it must be firm and aggressive. The clubhead will skid under the ball, kicking up the dirt that throws the ball into the air.

THE SHOT FROM A DIVOT

If your ball ends up in a relatively clean divot and there is no trouble between you and the green, the first choice is to hood or deloft a sand wedge or pitching wedge, position the ball back in your stance, and hit a low, driving shot that will fly and run to the putting surface. Be sure to set your weight left and your hands ahead of the ball at address; then keep them there as you strike down sharply on the ball.

Here's a tip that will help you play that pitch-and-run shot. Grip down on your club and set it more on the toe, turning the toe in so it will be sure to contact the ball first. The toe will not drag on you like the heel of the club will. Hitting the ball with the toe

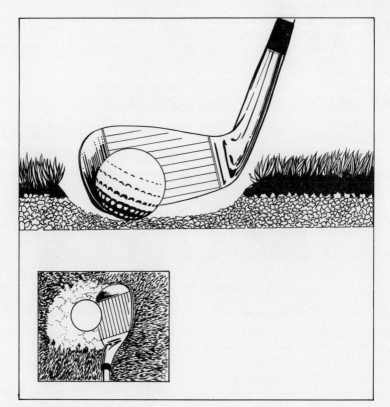

If the ball is in a divot, set the club more on the toe for a cleaner escape.

gets it going with less backspin, almost as if it has overspin, so it will run nicely onto the green.

Of course, if the ball is against the front wall of the divot or if it sits in a configuration that prevents you from playing the pitch-and-run, you must play the explosion shot just as if it were on hardpan, as I just described. That also is required, of course, if you have to loft the ball over an intervening hazard.

THE SHOT FROM A CUPPY LIE

If your ball is nestled into a bad lie, in a depression in the fairway or rough, your options are the same as above. With nothing in the way, drive it out with a sharply descending blow that will make it run to the green. If something is in the way, blast it, using the same technique as off hardpan. If you are confident and make an aggressive stroke, it will work.

THE SHORT PUNCH

Sometimes you face a situation in which you know you can't pitch the ball to the green and make it hold, either because of the firmness of the green or the location of the hole. If there is nothing but fairway between you and the pin, you can play the punch shot.

This situation occurs often on links courses, and it happened to me on the eighteenth at St. Andrews in the 1978 British Open. I had a 40-yard shot to the flag over the Valley of Sin, a large grassy hollow that fronts the eighteenth green. The green was baked out and would not hold a pitch, and I didn't want to try to run the ball all the way through the valley. The option was to punch a low wedge shot into the far wall of the valley and let it run up to the flag.

To play the shot, position the ball back in your stance, set your weight slightly to the left, and deloft the club. Hit down sharply on the back of the ball, keeping the wrists firm. The ball will fly low, strike the bank, bounce up, and roll toward the hole.

My shot in 1978 did just that, and I made the putt to finish in a tie for second.

THE BUMP SHOT

This is a shot you might face often, usually when you have knocked a shot over a green and down the bank behind it. Most greens slope from back to front, so now you either must pitch the ball up the bank to a green running away from you or go to your second option, which is the bump shot, where you bang the ball into the bank, bouncing and rolling it up onto the green.

To play the bump-and-run shot into a bank, choose a less-lofted club and let it bounce up the slope.

The texture of the ground between you and the green obviously dictates how you do this. If the ground is soft and/or the grass is high, you must take a club with enough loft—probably a 9-iron or pitching wedge—and carry the ball almost to the top of the slope, letting it bounce only once before it trickles onto the green.

If the ground is firmer and the grass is shorter, take a less lofted club and bang the ball into the middle of the slope, letting it bounce and roll the rest of the way onto the putting surface.

The shot is played by positioning the ball just back of middle in your stance, setting your weight slightly left and your hands ahead. Make a firm swing, keeping the clubhead going low through and after impact. It also helps if you use the right hand to rotate and turn the club over through impact, to help the ball run up the slope.

Your object is to get the ball close to the hole, of course, but if you are going to err, hit it too hard rather than too soft. If it goes well past the hole, you still have a chance to make a long putt. If you leave it short of the green, you face the same shot all over again.

Those are probably the most common special shots you will face around the green. As I said before, there are hundreds, maybe thousands, of others that can crop up in a lifetime of golf. Your ball will end up in places from which there is no prescribed technique for escape—perched in the grass on the edge of a bunker where you might have to make a baseball swing, stuck against a tree, partially submerged in water. The list is endless. You can play shots left-handed with a putter or one-handed and backhanded with an upside-down wedge. I once saw Gary Hallberg use that shot on the twelfth hole at Bay Hill when his ball was stuck in grass at the top of a deep bunker, and he holed it.

These shots require creativity. I can't instill it in you, nor can I teach you the shots. I'd just like to make you aware that there is more than one way to escape from any predicament, that you should consider every possibility (quickly, of course) before you give up and take a penalty stroke. Always consider the status of your round or match and weigh whether the reward is going to be worth the risk and the possible consequences of failure.

I'd also like to suggest that you have some fun in practice by trying crazy shots that might help you on the course. Once you have done them a few times, it's a lot easier to make the shots when it really counts.

You may be tired of my harping on practice. But you really can have fun in practice while you make yourself a better player, which is what the next and final chapter is all about.

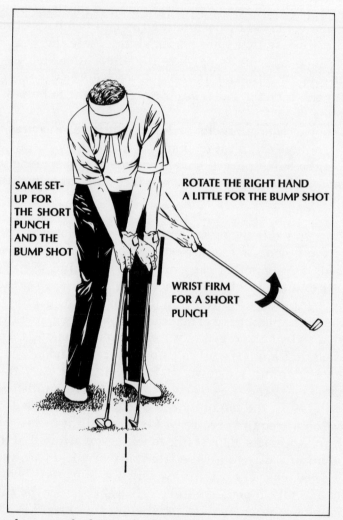

SAME SET-UP FOR THE SHORT PUNCH AND THE BUMP SHOT

ROTATE THE RIGHT HAND A LITTLE FOR THE BUMP SHOT

WRIST FIRM FOR A SHORT PUNCH

For the short punch shot or the bump-and-run, set the weight slightly left and make a firm-wristed stroke; for the bump-and-run, rotate the right hand a little through impact.

SPECIAL SHOTS IN BRIEF

- Recovery shots around the green are critical to scoring success.
- Learn what different kinds of shots you can hit with all your clubs.
- Be creative; examine your options and figure out a way to get the ball on the green.
- Take the easy way out; play the shot that will get you on the green with the least amount of penalty risk.
- Try funny shots in practice; then don't be afraid to use them on the course when the situation dictates.

7

MAKE YOUR
PRACTICE FUN

My dad owned his own course in North Carolina when I was a kid. Our house overlooked the eighteenth hole. One summer evening, about 5:30 after everybody had finished playing, I decided I wanted to work on my sand play. We didn't have a practice bunker, so I went to a bunker on the eighteenth, dumped out my bag of about 100 shag balls, and started whacking away. I was having a ball, playing all kinds of shots, burying balls in the front of the bunker and the back of the bunker and blasting them out, experimenting with various ways to get the ball out of the trap.

About 7:30 my dad closed up the club and came walking by on his way to the house. I am still beating balls, and by now I have virtually the entire bunker sitting up there on the green. There must have been a foot of sand spread over part of the putting surface.

Dad was livid. He made me go to the barn, get a shovel and broom and sweep all the sand back into the trap. But I didn't mind. It was worth it. I spent countless hours like that, experimenting and having fun at the same time, which is why today I can play almost any kind of bunker shot imaginable.

* * *

By now you may be tired of me talking about the necessity for practice. But, as I have said before, I don't know of any other way to get better at golf or anything else. Practice is important for a very simple reason—it creates skill, which creates confidence, which makes you a better player. Reading an instruction book or watching a videotape can give you knowledge, but it won't give you feel. To really learn a swing or a shot or a putt, to build the muscle memory that will let you repeat it consistently on the course, you have to practice it. Anything you do repetitiously becomes stored knowledge and produces a positive attitude, provided you do it well, of course. You can ingrain bad habits just as easily as good ones.

I often hear players say, "I'm not putting well. I need to make a few and I'll get my confidence back." I'm never sure which comes first, getting your confidence back or making a few putts. I know that after I hole a couple of putts I become more positive. As far as I'm concerned, that means I have to go to the practice green. If I start holing putts there, it should carry onto the course.

I don't know any other way to improve, whether you are building your game or trying to get out of a slump. And it works, not always immediately, but eventually. When I am putting poorly on the course and practicing a lot, I can have a good putting session but the results might not show up the first day. I'll go back for another good practice session, and maybe I won't putt well on the second day. I'll practice again and, boom, on the third day everything falls into place and I'm putting well again. If you can find a different way to do it, let me know. But I don't think you can.

I said early in this book that you can enjoy golf without playing it particularly well, without improving. That's the beauty of it. If you are satisfied at that point, bless you and have fun. But if you want to lower your score, you'll have to make an effort.

Actually, practice can be fun. And practicing your short game is especially fun. It is also rewarding, because you can see results immediately. You might take a lesson on the full swing every other day for a month and not see much improvement. But if you are chipping and pitching and playing out of the sand, using the correct method with some knowledge of what you are doing, improvement becomes quickly apparent. You can experiment, teach yourself new shots.

I'm not telling you to avoid practicing the long game. You must do both, but I think short-game practice is more important.

I can't tell you how often to practice. I'd tell you to do it every day for maximum results, but I assume you have a living to make and a family. But if you can get out at least two or three times a week for an hour or so each time during the season, you will reap the benefits.

How long should each session be? As long as you have time for without tiring. When you start to feel fatigued, your efficiency will drop and you will no longer benefit. That's another advantage of practicing your short game—it's not nearly as tiring to hit pitch shots or putts as it is to make full swings. That's why people usually get more out of an hour around the practice green than they do beating balls full out.

How do you make short-game practice fun?

For one thing, you can put a lot of variety into it, and that in itself makes it fun. If you think back to the last chapter, you will realize that there are a lot of funny shots to be made in golf. Working on them can be the spice of your practice time. I do it a lot.

Let me give you an example. One day at my club we had a lot of rain. Just below one of the bunkers is a low spot where water stands. The water in the middle of the puddle was probably 2 inches over a golf ball, so I could put balls just barely in the water at the edge or cover them completely. I put on my rain suit and spent 20 minutes hitting balls out of the puddle and splashing water in my face. (It's done basically the same as the sand shot, except you get wet a lot.)

One of the members walked by, and I could tell he thought I was crazy. But you never know when you might face such a shot. A perfect example is the thirteenth at Augusta, where if you miss the green short and right, the ball can roll down the bank into shallow water and be semisubmerged. You often can play it out of there, but I wouldn't want to try a shot like that in the Masters without having practiced it first.

So find yourself a puddle after a rain and start practicing. Your fellow members may chuckle, but they won't be laughing when you use the shot on the course to take their money.

In chapter 6 I explained how to hit the shot off hardpan, but you need to actually hit a lot of balls under those conditions

Practicing out of a puddle
after a rain may help you
later in an emergency on
the course.

before you develop confidence in the shot and the judgment that
tells you how hard you must swing. So look around your practice
area and find a worn-out spot, perhaps one where water often
stands so that it becomes hard and compacted. Then lay some
balls down and start blasting. You'll be surprised at how quickly
you start hitting good shots. Now, when you try it on the course,
there will be no surprises.

Practice putting with the leading edge of your sand wedge. All
you have to do is go to the putting green and putt one time around
the clock with your wedge and you will have learned the shot. It's
that easy. Then practice putting from the collar, the ball up
against the fringe or just off it in the higher grass. Now you will
have some confidence when you need to do it on the course.

How do you handle the routine shots, the bread-and-butter
strokes that can save you shots on every hole? How can practicing

those be fun? The best way is to play games. At the same time, practice as much as you can under pressure. That really isn't contradictory. You can do both at the same time and enjoy it a lot.

I simply mean that you should engage in competition while you practice, with yourself or somebody else. The putting green is the perfect place to chip or putt with a friend for small stakes. You are honing your physical and your competitive skills at the same time, and you're having fun. You also might win a dollar or two.

You also can play games alone, and I'm going to suggest just a few of them. You can vary the format and number of sets any way you wish. But keep track of your score. It forces you to be competitive with your toughest opponent—yourself. *You* are really the only person you ever play against in golf.

SAND PLAY

I have a very competitive game I play by myself in the bunker with 10 golf balls. You can use fewer or more. I put them in the practice bunker in 10 different lies, varying them in difficulty—a

Make a game of practicing from different lies out of a bunker, seeing how many times you can get up and down in two strokes.

perfect lie, a fried egg, a plugged lie, a ball in a rake rut, that sort of thing. Then I play all 10 out onto the green, take my putter, and try to make every putt. I figure my par is 25, which means I'm allowing myself 2½ strokes per ball. If I put all the balls in good lies, I might set my par at 22, or even 20, because I figure to hole 1 or 2 out of 10.

You can set your par at whatever number you think appropriate. I'll assure you that if you play this game often enough, your personal par will come down.

If your practice green is large enough, of course, you can vary the game by playing to different holes, either one at a time or within each set of 10 balls.

PITCHING

A variation of that bunker game is to take 10 balls back 50 yards and pitch them to a hole; then see how many of the putts you can make. Keep track of your score the first time, then do it again and again and watch your score come down. Try the same game but vary the distance from which you pitch each of the 10 balls. Or, especially if you have a number of holes in your practice green, pitch them to different pin placements.

When I was a boy, my dad showed me a practice game that improved my pitching game tremendously. Take a basket from the practice range, or a bucket or some other container, and pitch balls into it from, say, 30 yards away. When you get the feel for that, move back 10 yards or up 10 yards. This teaches you to pitch to a spot. You can even do that in your back yard, as long as you replace your divots.

Always keep track of your success ratio. How many times did you land in or near enough to the basket to call it a good shot? Keep trying to improve that ratio.

CHIPPING

Play the 10-ball game from the fringe of the green instead, chipping from various distances.

I play a chipping game that I enjoy very much. Put your 10 balls down on the fringe at some easy distance, say 35 feet, and give yourself a par: For example, I'll say that each chip should end up 2 feet from the hole, so that will be my par. Total footage for the 10 balls, then, will be 20 feet. Now I make the chips and figure up the total number of feet all the balls are from the hole. If the total is 15 feet, I am 5 under par. If it is 25 feet, I am 5 over and had better go do it again. You can assign your own par, of course, but don't be easy on yourself. The more demanding you are, the more you will improve.

PUTTING

Practice sets of 10 putts from various distances, just as you did your other shots. Try to make your third set, or your fifth, better than your first. Vary this by trying a set from 20 feet, then a set from 10 feet, and so on.

Put 10 balls (you may want to take fewer balls for this one at first) a foot from the hole and make them all. Then move back a foot and make them all. Keep moving back a foot at a time. Every time you miss, you must go forward to the last mark. Keep trying until you can make all the putts for 10 feet . . . or until it gets dark. But eventually you will be able to do it.

Don't limit either of these games to straight putts. Try to find spots on your putting green that break slightly and others that break severely. Play the games from both angles, left to right and right to left. Do the same on upslopes and downslopes.

WINTER GAMES

If you live in the north, where the courses shut down for a few months in the winter, there is still no need to lose your touch. There are some things you can do to be sharp as soon as the snow melts and the ground thaws. You can swing a weighted club in your garage or basement or living room (if your ceiling is high enough), just to keep the muscles strong and supple. Put a practice net in your garage or basement and hit all kinds of shots into it.

Especially, you can keep your short game in tune. Here are a couple of games that will do that: If you have a relatively smooth carpet, put down a coin and practice putting to it from various distances. Try to stop the ball right at the edge of the coin rather than rolling over it. Or put down a little piece of paper and try to stop the ball on it. That's great for your touch, your distance judgment, and your accuracy as well.

Practice chipping the ball the same way. If you can find 15 or 20 feet of carpeted space, you can do some quality work. (I would suggest that when spring comes you go to your practice green and do the same thing to adjust to the different speed. Hopefully your greens are faster than your carpet. Or you might even consider putting down a strip of outdoor carpet or artificial turf in your basement or garage to better approximate the normal green speed.)

Practice chipping and pitching with a plastic practice ball. You won't get the feel for distance but you can improve your stroke.

If you have room, make small shots with real balls, trying to pitch them onto a couch or chair. If you try this, however, be sure not to do what I did as a youngster. I was trying to pitch over the back of the couch and hold the ball on the cushion, and I caught one thin and broke Mom's best lamp. I was in real trouble for a while . . . but I also can now make that shot to a slick downhill green when it counts for a lot of money.

I even got in trouble in a hotel room once when I was considerably more than a kid. It was during a two-day rainout, I believe at the Memorial Tournament, and I had taken my clubs back to the room to regrip them. Afterward, I was checking them for size. There was a nice carpet on the floor, and soon I was chipping some balls over a chair onto a couch. Sure enough, I hit one thin, banged it into a big lamp, and broke two bulbs and the fixture itself. I had a little trouble explaining that one to the hotel engineer.

As you can imagine, there are endless ways to make a game out of practice, in your hotel room or at your course. Please find as many of them as you can. It has taken me many years of practice and thousands of rounds of competitive golf to master the short game, or at least come as close to it as I have. I don't expect you to reach the level that I and my fellow professionals have achieved. You don't play golf for a living. You play for fun, but you'll have more fun if you play better.

I hope this book has given you the knowledge that will help you play better. Now it's up to you to turn that knowledge into performance.

PRACTICE IN BRIEF

- Practice develops muscle memory, skill, confidence, and a positive approach.
- Have fun with your practice—work on a variety of special shots and play games when you practice the routine putts, chips, pitches, and sand shots.
- Be competitive in your practice, with a friend or against yourself; keep score to see your improvement.
- Practice as often as you can and as long as you can each session without tiring.